A CATHEDRAL
of
SUITABLE
MAGNIFICENCE

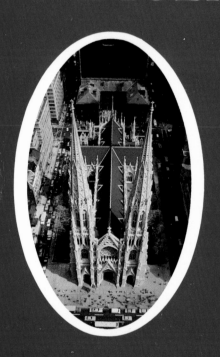

T. PATRICK'S CATHEDRAL
NEW YORK

Margaret Carthy, O.S.U.

A CATHEDRAL
OF SUITABLE MAGNIFICENCE

A Cathedral of Suitable Magnificence

St. Patrick's Cathedral New York

by Margaret Carthy, o.s.u.

MICHAEL GLAZIER, INC.
Wilmington, Delaware

ABOUT THE AUTHOR

Margaret Carthy, O.S.U. studied American Church History at the Catholic University of America, receiving the degrees of Master of Arts and Doctor of Philosophy, respectively. She has held administrative positions at Columbia University and The University of Maryland, and served on the editorial staff of *The New Catholic Encyclopedia*, specializing in American Church History. She is the author of a number of historical works including "English Influences on Early American Catholicism," in *Historical Records and Studies*; *Catholicism in English-Speaking Lands*; and various articles in *The New Catholic Encyclopedia*

First published in 1984 by Michael Glazier Inc., 1723 Delaware Avenue, Wilmington, Delaware 19806 • © 1984 by Margaret Carthy, O.S.U. All rights reserved. • Library of Congress Card Catalog Number: 83-82667 • International Standard Book Numbers (0-89453-372-X, Cloth) and (0-89453-373-8, Paper) • Typography by Richard Reinsmith • Cover design by Charles Roth • Printed in the United States of America.

Acknowledgments

The publisher wishes to thank the following for use of illustrations: The Library of Congress, pages 27 and 97. National Portrait Gallery, Smithsonian Institution, page 39. Walter Sturges, Renwick rending of Cathedral, page 31. Archives of the Archdiocese of New York, pages 31, 49, 59, 63, 105, 115, 118, 133 and 137. Archives of St. Patrick's Cathedral, pages 41, 71, 81, 127, 139, cover i and cover iv.

Cover photographs by C.H. Conroy

Table of Contents

Foreword

"To one it is given to begin, to another to carry on and by God's blessing to make perfect." These were the words of Archbishop John Hughes in 1858 at the ground-breaking for Saint Patrick's Cathedral which he said would be a house of prayer "of suitable magnificence for the Church of New York."

Since that ceremony one hundred and twenty-four years ago, the people of the Church of New York have put much faith-filled, loving care and skillful talent into Saint Patrick's Cathedral. They have made it truly the Parish Church of our City and of our Archdiocese.

During the period of construction, there were many difficulties and delays, as the Civil War engulfed the nation. Finally in 1879, John Cardinal McCloskey, carrying on what Archbishop Hughes had begun, opened and dedicated the Cathedral. It was without spires, and the Lady Chapel had not been built. Yet it received unprecedented praise in newspaper accounts of the day. Its exterior was likened to that of the Cologne Cathedral and its interior to the Cathedral of Amiens.

Over the years, the beauty of Saint Patrick's has been further enhanced. During the time of Archbishop Michael Corrigan, the tall spires, which are the hallmark of the Cathedral, were erected. He also made plans for the Lady Chapel which was completed by his successor, John Cardinal Farley, as the first Mass was offered there on Christmas Day, 1906.

In the time of Patrick Cardinal Hayes and Francis Cardinal Spellman, despite the upheavals of war and the difficulties of economic depression, programs of restoration and renewal in the interior and exterior of the Cathedral were completed.

In the years following the Second Vatican Council, renovations were made to conform to the new liturgical requirements. In very recent times, during the 1970's, a thorough restoration of the exterior and interior of the Cathedral was undertaken. The addition of outside lighting for the Cathedral's steeples and facades has highlighted its majestic and comforting presence in the evening hours. Similar lighting, focused on the statue of the Blessed Mother looking down on Madison Avenue, has manifested the architectural beauty of the Lady Chapel.

In the 1980's, as Saint Patrick's enters its second century of worship of God and loving service to God's people, the Cathedral, which was the dream of Archbishop Hughes, is known throughout the world as a place of beauty and peace in the midst of a bustling city.

At the heart and soul of Saint Patrick's Cathedral there is much more than architectural beauty and historical events. What makes it alive and well is the people who come to worship and to find God. This centennial history of Sister Margaret Carthy attempts to record in some detail this special aspect of Saint Patrick's, its role as a parish church in midtown New York. Under the leadership of four successive Rectors, the Cathedral parish has adapted to ever-changing conditions. It has developed a flexible and resourceful vitality and the ability to respond to the mobility of the people and the circumstances of history.

In the early days, the parishioners of Saint Patrick's formed a close worshipping community. They were part of a neighborhood. They knew each other. They knew their priests, and their priests knew them and ministered to them in all the joys and sorrows of life.

In the parish school, their children were educated by a devoted faculty composed of Brothers of the Christian Schools, who were known to everyone as the Christian Brothers, the Sisters of Charity, who carried on the vibrant heritage of Mother Seton, and by dedicated lay men and women.

The parish was truly the center of the lives of the people. A number of societies met a diversity of spiritual, social and cultural needs. The Cathedral Free Circulating Library, which opened its doors in 1888, soon became more than a parish facility as it established a number of branches in other populated areas of the city.

In later years, the geographical area of the Cathedral Parish became less and less a family-oriented neighborhood. As midtown Manhattan became a center of business and commerce, the families moved to residential areas of Manhattan, the Bronx, Brooklyn and to the suburbs. Still, the Cathedral Parish continued its mission to people — to God's own people. The worship of Almighty God, the availability of the Sacraments of Salvation, the preaching of the Gospel of Christ, the sharing of His teaching through Instruction Classes — all have been and will remain the work of the people and the priests of Saint Patrick's.

By the centenary year 1979 an increasing number of midtown workers were looking to the Cathedral as their weekday parish. More than 1,500 persons participate at Holy Mass each weekday. On Sunday, Mass attendance averages between five and six thousand people, of whom about ninety percent are visitors to New York. In addition to those who attend Mass, a very large number of men, women and children of every faith come to the Cathedral to say a brief prayer and to find a moment of peace in the midst of their lives. All of them, whether visitors to the City or New Yorkers, have come to look upon Saint Patrick's as home.

In its second century, the Cathedral Parish has established a number of challenging goals for the years ahead. These will only further enhance its legacy of service and worship to Almighty God. I am confident that Sister Margaret Carthy's thoughtful and scholarly view of the history, past and present, of Saint Patrick's Cathedral will help guide the parish into the future with a great spirit of Christian hope.

Terence Cardinal Cooke
August 15, 1983

Acknowledgments

As the aftermath of a conversation between Cardinal Terence Cooke and Monsignor John Tracy Ellis during the centenary celebration of New York's St. Patrick's Cathedral, the writer was offered, and accepted, a commission to research and write a scholarly history of this well-known New York landmark. Since its opening in 1879, the Fifth Avenue St. Patrick's has been not only the principal church of the archdiocese in which the residential archbishop has his throne, it has also served as parish church for residents in the vicinity. It is on the latter aspect of the cathedral's history that this volume has attempted to place major emphasis since existing works include only a perfunctory treatment of it.

Many people have provided assistance and encouragement during the course of this effort. Thus, in the first instance, grateful acknowledgment is made of Cardinal Cooke's gracious interest in and support of this project. Sincere thanks are also due to Monsignor James F. Rigney, Rector of St. Patrick's Cathedral, for his many kindnesses, including the reading of the final draft of the manuscript and the pointing out of a number of needed corrections. To Monsignor Ellis a supreme debt of gratitude is owed for improving the work by his critical reading of the manuscript, chapter by chapter as each was completed, as well as for his continued friendship, guidance and encouragement over the many years since he directed the writer's graduate studies at The Catholic University of America.

Special thanks are also recorded for the courtesies afforded the writer by Monsignor Edward J. Mitty, Executive Director of the Trustees of St. Patrick's Cathedral, with special mention of his secretary, Miss Rosella P. Glynn, for her kind acts of supererogation. Others who rendered valuable assistance by providing relevant data include Sister Marguerita Smith, O.P., Archivist of the Archdiocese of New York; Sister Patricia A. Walsh, S.C., Secretary of the Congregation of the Sisters of Charity of New York; Brother Frederick Altenburg, F.S.C., Archivist for the Brothers of the Christian Schools; The Reverend William Collins of St. Joseph's Seminary, Dunwoodie; Monsignor John M. Connolly, Vice Chancellor of the Archdiocese of New York, and his staff member, Sister Julia Miriam Schneider, S.C. For the kindly assistance and hospitality extended by the Reverend John J. Tierney as Archivist of the Archdiocese of Baltimore, and that of Mr. Anthony Zito, Archivist of The Catholic University of America, the writer is sincerely appreciative.

Acknowledgment is also made of the debt of gratitude owed to the various librarians of the Mother Augustine Gill Library of the College of New Rochelle, as well as those of St. Joseph's Seminary, Dunwoodie, and the personnel of the New York Public Library on Fifth Avenue in New York City. To Mrs. Nora Lawler (nee Maguire), an alumna of Cathedral School, special thanks are recorded for her generous efforts in behalf of this project. Finally, the writer acknowledges with deep appreciation the prayerful support of the members of her Ursuline Community of New Rochelle, together with the various kinds of material help which they freely offered; among the latter the services of Sister Jane Frances Cuddy were invaluable.

Margaret Carthy, o.s.u.

A CATHEDRAL
OF SUITABLE MAGNIFICENCE

Abbreviations

CHAPTER I

Catholicism in Early New York

It was to the future of Catholicism in the United States, particularly in that part of it known as the "Empire State," that Archbishop John Hughes looked when on October 3, 1850, the new metropolitan spoke for the first time in public of his dream of a new cathedral of suitable magnificence for the Church of New York.[1] During the more than sixty years since John Carroll had been appointed the first Bishop of Baltimore, a diocese then coterminous with the United States, the Catholic population of the country had grown and flourished. Such was the progress of the Church in the new Republic that in 1808 Carroll was named the first American archbishop, with New York one of the four new dioceses established as suffragans of Baltimore.[2] However, it was not until about thirty years later that the really constructive phase of the history of Catholicism in that metropolis began with the arrival in New York of John Hughes to serve as coadjutor to the aging Bishop John Dubois.

As emigrants from County Tyrone, Ireland, the Hughes family in 1818 had settled in Pennsylvania, where young John worked at various tasks in the quarries, mending roads and as a gardener. Admitted to Mount Saint Mary's Seminary at Emmitsburg, Maryland, in 1820, he was ordained on October 15, 1826, by Bishop Henry Conwell for the Diocese of Philadelphia.

After brief intervals of service at St. Augustine's in Philadelphia and a parish in Bedford, Hughes returned to Philadelphia in January, 1827, as pastor of St. Joseph's. Except
for a few months in the spring and summer of 1827, during
which he was at St. Mary's in Philadelphia, he served at St.
Joseph's until April 1832, when he was assigned as pastor of
Philadelphia's newly dedicated Church of St. John. Precognized in 1837 as titular Bishop of Basileopolis and coadjutor, with the right of succession, of New York, he was
consecrated there on January 7, 1838, in old St. Patrick's
Cathedral on Mott Street. Unrelenting where principles
were concerned, Hughes early acquired the reputation of a
fighter, one which he retained to the end of his career. His
handling of the trustee problem, which was at a critical stage
when the young coadjutor arrived at St. Patrick's, was an
early example of the decisive firmness which characterized
the eventful life of the first Archbishop of New York.[3] A
brief review of the history of Catholic presence in New York
will shed some light on the situation there at the time of
Hughes' arrival in that city.

During colonial times, and particularly after the over-
throw of King James II of England in 1688 when drastic
penal laws were imposed in the American colonies as elsewhere in the English-speaking world, very few Catholics
were to be found in New York. However, the advent of the
American Revolution and the inauguration of a policy of
toleration presaged the dawn of better days for Catholics.
Although an uncertain tradition holds that Mass was
offered in New York City as early as 1775, it was probably
only after the British evacuation of the city in 1783 that the
Jesuit missionary known as Father Ferdinand Farmer
openly entered New York and offered Mass wherever
accommodations could be secured.[4] At that time, and until
the passage of the law of 1784 in New York State, the few
Catholics to be found there were without even the prospect

of a church of their own. Under the Act of 1784 which permitted any religious denomination to organize as a body corporate to manage its own affairs, a small group of Catholic laymen, with the help of the French consul, Hector St. John de Crevecoeur, on June 10, 1785, incorporated as "The Trustees of the Roman Catholic Church in the City of New York."[5]

Through the initiative of this group, a small congregation of Irish, French, Dutch, German, Spanish, and Portuguese Catholic residents was organized, funds collected, and a site on Barclay Street procured for the erection of New York's first Catholic Church, St. Peter's in lower Manhattan. In keeping with an American tradition of Protestant origin, these lay trustees had organized independently of ecclesiastical authority and considered themselves to be the true administrators of the parish with the right to choose and dismiss their pastors. Carroll, at this time possessing only the powers of superior of the American missions, had permitted the incorporation, granting faculties as rector of St. Peter's to the Irish Capuchin Charles Whelan and, some months later, to another Irish Capuchin Andrew Nugent, as Whelan's assistant.[6] Nugent, a better preacher than Whelan, soon won the support of the trustees who demanded that Whelan resign and leave the city. Carroll then warned the trustees that if they instituted legal action to rid themselves of Whelan, they would be without a pastor since he would not grant faculties to any priest supporting such action.[7] Ignoring this warning, the trustees continued their attack against Whelan until the latter, greatly discouraged, quit the city, leaving Carroll no alternative but to appoint Nugent temporary pastor with faculties "*usque ad revocationem.*"[8] Throughout this period of dissension, construction of the church continued, making possible the opening of St. Peter's, although not completely finished, on November 4, 1786.

Unfortunately, peace did not reign for long at St. Peter's where controversy again broke out, this time between the trustees and Nugent. When the latter defied the authority of Carroll, the trustees instituted legal proceedings against Nugent which resulted in his removal from St. Peter's.[9] With the appointment of the Dominican William O'Brien as pastor there in October 1787, the congregation entered upon a period of growth and development so that upon his retirement from St. Peter's in August 1807, Catholicism in New York appeared to be firmly established. Moreover, by 1802 Catholics had begun to enter public service in the person of Andrew Morris, a trustee of St. Peter's who served as assistant alderman of the First Ward in 1802 and continued as alderman until 1806.[10] In that year, Francis Cooper, also of St. Peter's, was the first Catholic to be elected to the New York State Assembly.[11]

When Pope Pius VII divided the See of Baltimore in 1808, erecting New York as one of the four new suffragans of Baltimore, Father Luke Concanen, an Irish Dominican then resident in Rome, was named for New York.[12] Following his consecration in Rome on April 24, 1808, Concanen's several attempts to embark for New York from Italian ports were frustrated by conditions resulting from the Napoleonic Wars. Seeing no prospect of arriving in his see in the immediate future, Concanen wrote on July 23, 1808, to request Carroll to appoint to New York a vicar general with full powers of administration.[13] Carroll's choice fell upon the German Jesuit, Anthony Kohlmann, who arrived in New York in October 1808, accompanied by his fellow Jesuits Father Benedict Fenwick and four scholastics, James Wallace, Michael White, James Redmond and Adam Marshall.[14] Within a matter of months, so remarkable was the growth of religious observance in the parish that St. Peter's became inadequate to accommodate the expanding congregation. This, and the desire to provide a structure suitable to serve as a cathedral for New York's new bishop, led to the decision to erect the Cathedral of St. Patrick in what was then the suburban section of the city. The site decided upon was at the northwestern corner of Prince and Mott Streets, on property which had been secured for a Catholic cemetery in 1801 and 1803 by "The Trustees for the Roman Catholic Congregation of St. Peter's Church in the City of New York."[15] There, on June 8, 1809, in the presence of more than 3,000 persons, the cornerstone was laid by Kohlmann, officiating in his capacity as vicar general of the diocese.

Hopes for an early completion of the cathedral were doomed to disappointment as precarious funding continued to be a source of worry to the trustees. In addition, the Embargo and Non-intercourse Acts, and finally the War of 1812 between the United States and England, produced the hard times that are the concomitant of every war. New York, as the leading commercial center, felt the effects of the war even more than the rest of the country. The population of the city decreased by more than 2,000 between 1810-1813, while in 1814 the revenues of the port dropped down to little more than $500,000.[16] Even more disheartening to the Catholics of New York than these financial problems, was the news of the sudden death of Bishop Concanen who, having secured passage on the ship *Frances of Salem* scheduled to sail for America on June 17, 1810, was not permitted to embark until some real or feigned flaw in his passport was rectified. Two days after the ship sailed without him, Concanen died and was buried in the vault of his order in the Dominican Church of San Domenico Maggiore, Naples.[17] When, more than three months later, the sad news reached New York, Father Kohlmann celebrated a solemn requiem Mass in St. Peter's Church on the first Sunday in October, deviating from the rubrics of the Church in order to accommodate the congregation, few of whom would have been free to attend the service if held on a weekday.[18]

Because of the Holy See's decision not to name anyone to

vacant bishoprics as long as Pius VII was held a prisoner by
Napoleon, the appointment of a successor to Concanen was
delayed until late in 1814. Accordingly, the power to name
an administrator for the vacant Diocese of New York lay
with the bishops of the United States. Their choice, logically
enough, was Father Anthony Kohlmann whose services had
already proved of immense value to the Church of New
York and continued so until his recall early in 1815. Meanwhile, with the liberation of Pius VII and his return to Rome
in May 1814, it became evident that action would soon be
taken to name the second Bishop of New York. Once again
an Irish Dominican, the scholarly prior of San Clemente in
Rome, John Connolly, was chosen for the vacant see.[19]
Although he was consecrated in Rome on November 6,
1814, the new bishop did not arrive in his see until
November 25, 1815.[20]

Meanwhile, Father Fenwick, in charge of New York
following Kohlmann's recall and return to Maryland (January 1815), succeeded in advancing construction on the
cathedral which, although still unfinished, was ready for
dedication that spring. When May 4, 1815, the feast of the
Ascension, was selected for the ceremony, Archbishop Carroll was invited to preside, but the aging father of the
American hierarchy was obliged to decline. Instead, Bishop
Jean Cheverus of Boston performed the ceremony, making
New York's new cathedral the first church in the United
States to be dedicated to Ireland's patron saint. Six months
later upon his arrival in New York, Connolly was to dis-
cover that with his cathedral he not only had inherited a
substantial debt, the interest payments on which were to be
a continuing drain on the slender resources of the parish,
but a host of other problems as well. Moreover, the death on
December 3, 1815, of the venerable father of the American
hierarchy, John Carroll, came before Connolly had a
chance to visit Baltimore, thus depriving both churchmen of

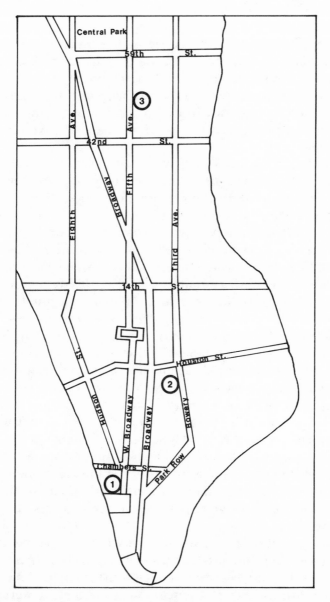

1) St. Peter's Church (1786), (New York City's First Catholic Church)
2) (First) St. Patrick's Cathedral (1815); 3) (Present) St. Patrick's
Cathedral (1879)

the opportunity to exchange views. In a letter written on December 7 to Carroll's successor, Archbishop Leonard Neale, Connolly stated "I have long admired and esteemed him [Carroll] on account of his learning, zeal, and piety. His death will be regretted in Europe as well as in America, particularly at Rome, where his Holiness often spoke to me of him..."[21]

In 1815, the Diocese of New York included the whole of New York State and the northern half of New Jersey, where there were only three churches and four priests to serve a Catholic population of about 15,000.[22] During the ensuing years, an extraordinary increase in immigration through the port of New York brought the Catholic population of New York City alone to an estimated 20,000, of whom the majority were Irish. In sharp contrast, the clergy list during Connolly's administration provided all too few priests to minister to this ever-increasing flock. Moreover, the heavy burden of debt inherited by the new bishop discouraged him from any thought of establishing a seminary as a means of augmenting his clergy. As a consequence, recruits had to be sought from abroad as well as within the United States. Unfortunately, those recruited included a number who would subsequently play prominent roles in the bitter trustee controversies that developed in 1818, casting a shadow over the remainder of Connolly's adminstration and beyond. Before detailing the history of this era of violent agitation in church affairs, it seems appropriate to first review some of the more positive accomplishments of the Connolly administration.

With the closing of their respective schools by the Jesuits, Ursulines and Trappists on the eve of Connolly's arrival in New York, Catholics there were left with the one free school attached to St. Peter's Church. It was not long, however, before a free school was opened in the basement of St. Patrick's which, by 1817, had a registration of more than

240, including boys and girls. When increasing enrollment rendered the space inadequate, temporary quarters were found for the girls' school until such time as plans could be executed for the erection of a new school building. By 1819, new school facilities were ready for the more than 350 children enrolled in 1820, a number which had grown to over 400 three years later.[23] Under a New York State law of 1805, a Common School Fund had been set up, the income from which was to be apportioned among the school districts of the State. At this time, although public schools were to be found in other parts of the State, New York City's school system was entirely of private and religious origin. Nevertheless, appropriations from this fund were distributed to the city's denominational schools and to the schools established by the Free School Society, a private corporation organized in 1805 "for the Education of such poor Children as do not belong to or are not provided for by any Religious Society." St. Peter's Free School, in existence since 1800 and by 1805 the largest of the city's denominational schools, successfully petitioned the legislature for a share of the fund, receiving in May 1806 a little more than $1,500, the first public aid to Catholic education.[24] For no known reason, it was not until 1814 that St. Peter's began to receive regularly a portion of this school fund, while at St. Patrick's public money in support of their school was received regularly between 1817-1823.

In 1824, however, under a state law the Common Council of the City of New York was given full powers to distribute the School Fund as that body deemed proper. As a consequence, action was taken to prevent the distribution of any portion of the School Fund to the schools of religious societies, thus leaving the Public School Society[25] as the principal beneficiary. By 1840, opposition by Protestants conducting schools to the Public School Society's monopoly of public funding had practically disappeared, despite the fact that this private corporation's stated purpose was "to inculcate the sublime truths of religion and morality contained in the Holy Scriptures."[26] It was left to John Hughes, consecrated in New York in 1838 as coadjutor to Bishop Dubois, to provide that diocese with strong leadership not only in the struggle against trusteeism and in the fight for a share of the common school fund, but also in the recurrent outbreaks of nativist bigotry against Catholics that unfortunately did not disappear entirely from the American scene until the last half of the twentieth century.

From the beginning, the cathedral schools opened by Connolly were staffed by lay teachers, working under the close supervision of a committee regularly appointed by the trustees; any misconduct on the part of the teachers could result in removal by vote of the Board of Trustees. Laymen, selected and appointed by the trustees, continued to staff the boys' school until 1849, when the Christian Brothers were officially placed in charge.[27] Much earlier, favorable circumstances had decreed that the teaching in the girls' school at the cathedral would be taken over by the Emmitsburg Sisters of Charity. As early as 1817, Connolly had applied to Emmitsburg for several of Mother Seton's daughters to take care of the orphans of his diocese. Elizabeth Seton, who could refuse nothing to the city of her birth and conversion to the faith, responded by sending Sisters Rose White, Cecilia O'Conway and Felicite Brady to New York to take up residence in a small frame building on Prince Street that became the first Catholic orphan asylum in the diocese. In the same year, the New York Roman Catholic Benevolent Society was incorporated for the purpose of providing financial support for the establishment.[28] As the number of orphans confided to the sister's care increased, additional sisters came from Emmitsburg not only to assist at the orphanage but, in 1820 at Connolly's request, to take over the teaching in the girls' school of the cathedral.[29] To the prelate's unremitting efforts to support these institutions and to find an adequate number of good priests so that he would not wear himself out performing parish duties, was added the problem of dealing with recalcitrant trustees. The latter at times not only withheld the payments owed to the clergy, but even those to the bishop, whose salary in February 1817 was three months in arrears.[30] It beame clear to Connolly that some action to correct this must be taken.

Up to this time St. Patrick's and St. Peter's were incorporated conjointly under a general law passed in 1813 which was designed to supersede the original Act of 1784. The purpose of the 1813 law was to place the control of temporal affairs of religious societies in the hands of three to nine trustees elected by the male members of the church who were stated worshippers thereof, and who supported it for at least one year preceding the election. The act further declared that the salary of the minister was to be decided by a vote of the congregation and ratified by the trustees.[31] Connolly, convinced that the existing board of trustees was unwilling or unable to place the two churches on a sound financial basis, succeeded in procuring separate incorporation for the cathedral church with a board of trustees loyal to himself. The charter of incorporation, "The Trustees of St. Patrick's Cathedral in the City of New York," provided that the trustees were to be elected annually from among the pewholders or stated worshippers of the church. Three new trustees were to be elected each year on Easter Monday to replace three whose terms would expire, notice of the election to be given during divine service on the three Sundays preceding.[32] It is interesting to note, parenthetically , that this system of lay trusteeism remains to this day in New York's old and new Cathedral of St. Patrick, although it was eventually abolished elsewhere throughout the diocese.

When Connolly moved to get similar control of the board

of trustees at St. Peter's, a bitter struggle with racial over-
tones ensued between those upholding the bishop and those
supporting the trustees and rebellious priests. Siding with
the trustees were Peter Malou, the Belgian Jesuit at St.
Peter's and Father William Taylor, an Irish priest who was a
member of the cathedral staff (1818-1820). The bishop had
the support of his fellow Dominicans, Thomas Carbry, who
left New York in 1819, and Charles Ffrench of St. Peter's
Church who became leader of the party upholding the
bishop after Carbry's departure. When nationalistic feelings
were appealed to, the Malou party had the support of those
who approved what the Irish considered a preponderance of
French influence in ecclesiastical affairs in the United
States. On the other hand, the Irish Dominicans attracted
support from the growing number of Irish immigrants in the
city. In the ensuing years, conflicting reports of the heated
controversies in New York reached not only the metropolitan, Archbishop Ambrose Maréchal, S.S., of Baltimore,
but the authorities in Rome as well.[33] Thus, in July 1821,
Rome took action, notifying Connolly that he was "to
exhort Father Ffrench to leave the diocese... within three
months from the receipt of this letter." With respect to
Father Malou, the bishop was instructed to "give orders to
leave the diocese at once, under pain of being deprived of all
faculties and of suspension *a divinis.*"[34] Although Ffrench
promptly obeyed the command of Rome, Malou stayed on
in New York where, after the death of Connolly on February 5, 1825, the Jesuit resumed his priestly duties at St.
Peter's following restoration of his faculties by order of
Rome.[35]

Two days before his death, Bishop Connolly had
appointed as vicar general and, in the event of his death,
administrator for New York, Irish-born Father John
Power, an assistant at St. Peter's since 1819 and its pastor
since 1822. During the months that passed while Rome

deliberated on the choice of someone to fill the vacancy in New York, Power exercised his powers as administrator and appointed to the rectorship of the cathedral, the Reverend Thomas C. Levins, whose first baptismal entry was dated May 22, 1825. A former Jesuit who had taught at Georgetown College before he left the society in October 1824, Levins' competence as a pulpit orator soon won for him the esteem of the people. In February 1826, Power named as co-rector of the cathedral [36] Father William Taylor who had arrived in New York from Boston the preceding December ostensibly to proceed directly to France, though in fact he remained another year in the United States. The period of Power's administration saw the opening in May 1826 of a third church in the city when a former Presbyterian place of worship on Sheriff Street was remodelled for Catholic use, becoming the Church of St. Mary with the Reverend Hatton Walsh as its first rector.[37]

These years were also marked by the establishment of New York's first Catholic weekly, the *Truth Teller*, which appeared on April 2, 1825, under the imprint of William E. Andrews & Company, 95 Maiden Lane. Local Catholic news, however, did not appear in the paper until the sixth issue, May 7, when it carried a notice of a coming sermon by Dr. Power for the benefit of the orphan asylum. With this issue, the earlier imprint of Andrews & Company gave way to "Printed by the Proprietors George Pardow and William Denman at the office. Collect opposite Canal Street." In 1830, Pardow sold his interest in the paper to Denman who continued as its owner until 1855 when it was consolidated with the *Irish American*.[38]

While the episcopal appointment to New York was still pending, Power not only became a popular candidate among his flock, but also enjoyed the support of Bishop John England of Charleston. However, the majority of the American hierarchy favored either Benedict Fenwick or

John Dubois for the vacancy in New York.[39] Arriving in the summer of 1826, the Roman bulls officially named John Dubois , then President of Mount Saint Mary's College at Emmitsburg. Born in Paris, Dubois was among the estimated 30,000 priests who joined the "Church of exile" during the French Revolution rather than take the oath supporting the Civil Constitution of the Clergy which had been condemned by Pius VI early in 1791. In August of that year, Dubois arrived at Norfolk, Virginia, where he soon became an American citizen. In 1807, he established a preparatory seminary in Emmitsburg, Maryland, which later expanded into Mount Saint Mary's College and Seminary for the education of theological students and laymen. Despite early difficulties, this institution prospered, numbering among its alumni such leading members of the American hierarchy as John McCloskey, John Hughes and John B. Purcell. It was Dubois who also provided the help Mother Elizabeth Seton needed to found her first convent of Sisters of Charity in 1809.

Bowing to the mandate of Rome, Dubois resigned his office as president of the college and on Sunday, October 29, 1826, was consecrated third Bishop of New York in the cathedral of Baltimore. Archbishop Maréchal presided and was assisted by Power from New York and Henry Conwell, Bishop of Philadelphia.[40] The sermon for the occasion, delivered by Father William Taylor, was, to put it mildly, extremely tactless in its references to the vexations and troubles in store in New York for the new bishop. Referring to Rome's unfortunate predilection for placing foreign prelates over a flock almost exclusively Irish, Taylor warned Dubois that his appointment "was a bold and hazardous experiment and one which would or might sever the people from the centre of unity..."[41] Fortunately Dubois was undismayed by this prophecy of doom and the following Sunday saw him installed in New York in his cathedral church. In accepting Power's surrender of the government of the diocese into his hands, Dubois used the occasion to warn his flock that there should be "but one heart and one soul between the Bishop, his clergy, and the congregation," and that by acting in unison "the Catholics of New York might almost work miracles."[42]

Although no miracles marked the years of Dubois' administration, the bishop's keen interest in expanding educational opportunities for Catholic youths, his efforts to find a sufficient number of good priests for his growing flock, and his plans to provide additional churches to meet their needs did result in a measure of success. In 1830, additional sisters arrived from Emmitsburg to open an academy for girls, but Dubois' negotiations with an Irish brotherhood for the establishment of a similar school for boys were frustrated by trustee opposition. Since the controversy centered chiefly around the issue of who should hold title to the proposed school property, the project had to be abandoned since the brothers were unwilling to accept lay interference.[43]

The new orphan asylum accommodating 160 children, completed under Power's administration, continued to prosper under the direction of the Sisters of Charity and the support of the bishop. Seeing the need for a refuge for children left with only one parent without proper means of caring for them, Dubois brought about the establishment of a "half-orphan" asylum also staffed by the sisters. When Dubois acquired the deed for Christ Episcopal Church on Ann Street and dedicated it for Catholic use on July 15, 1827, he gave New York City its fourth church for a Catholic population which the bishop estimated was at least 35,000.[44] In 1829, Dubois traveled in Europe, where his pleas for financial help met with some response from agencies such as the Congregation de Propaganda Fide in Rome, the French Society for the Propagation of the Faith and the Ludwig-Missionsverein.[45]

Meanwhile, the increasing number of Catholics, the

growing number of their churches and the emergence of articulate leaders had not gone unnoticed by American Protestants whose deep-seated suspicion of popery was only exceeded by their implacable hatred of the "Paddies of the pope." By 1832, this opposition to Catholicism took organized form in the meetings of the New York Protestant Association whose president, the Reverend William C. Brownlee, used the Association's journal, *The Protestant*, and other public forums to expose the perils of Romanism. Such attacks were boldly and capably answered by a number of Catholic champions, among the ablest of whom were Fathers Levins, Power and Felix Varela. However, after some months, the priests announced that they could no longer debate with one whose substitutes for argument were "falsehood, ribald words, gross invective, disgusting calumny, and the recommendation of an obscene tale."[46]

The formation in 1835 of the Native American Democratic Association, whose platform pledged opposition to foreigners in office, to pauper and criminal immigration, and to the Catholic Church, supplied the political impulse which in 1845 brought into being the Native American Party. A flood of anti-Catholic books also marked these years, the most notorious of which was printed in New York in 1836. Titled *Awful Disclosures of the Hotel Dieu Nunnery of Montreal* and ostensibly from the pen of Maria Monk, a pseudo ex-nun, this book was deemed by the Protestant historian Ray Allen Billington "the most influential single work of American nativistic propaganda in the period preceding the Civil War."[47] Violent street attacks in the summer of 1824 by Orangemen against the Catholics of Greenwich Village, then a suburb of the city, were but an early portent of worse evils to come. When work began on the Church of St. Joseph in the same village, the men of the parish had to stand guard at night to prevent destruction of the building.[48] The burning of St. Mary's Church on Sheriff

Street in 1831 was undoubtedly the work of an enemy of Catholicism and, although never clearly determined, the destruction by fire of the Nyack seminary, a cherished project of Dubois, was probably the work of a bigot. Even St. Patrick's Cathedral was the object of a planned attack in 1835, but fortunately this was abandoned when the Catholics of the city assembled for its defense.[49]

During these same years, in addition to the rising Protestant hostility to the Church, Dubois also had to contend with a prolonged conflict with the trustees of his own cathedral. The trouble began in 1834 when the trustees disputed the bishop's right to give the deciding vote on a question over which the board members were equally divided, namely, whether or not another priest should be engaged to serve the cathedral congregation. Having cast his vote in the affirmative, Dubois was attacked by the opposition who, led by James Shea, denied "the validity of any vote given in this Board by any person whatsoever, other than a Trustee of this Cathedral."[50] The conflict escalated when Dubois suspended and subsequently removed Levins, the pastor of the cathedral, who on several past occasions had incurred his superior's displeasure. This time, the trouble arose over an offensive note written by Levins to Dubois declaring: "if you wish for war, at once declare it, I am ready."[51] Matters worsened when Dubois appointed Father Peter Walsh in Levins' place and the trustees retaliated by denying the newcomer the customary salary to which a pastor was entitled, voting him merely that of an assistant. Dubois then threatened to interdict the cathedral if the trustees continued "to retain Rev. Mr. Levins whose faculties are withdrawn" and "to withhold the customary salary to which Rev. Mr. Walsh becomes entitled by his appointment." Even after Levins wrote to the trustees declining any salary after April 1835 and subsequently moved to a house not far from the cathedral, the trustees continued to annoy Dubois with requests for Levins' restoration and went so far as to appoint the suspended priest rector of the cathedral school.

Finding himself exhausted by these years of struggle, the seventy-two-year-old prelate in November 1837, had sought and obtained a coadjutor in the person of John Hughes who, after his consecration in St. Patrick's in January 1838, soon entered the battle to end trustee domination in church affairs. Calling a meeting of the pewholders of the cathedral on February 24, 1839, the coadjutor appealed over the heads of the trustees to the congregation. When the audience unanimously adopted a preamble and resolutions introduced by Hughes, it became only a matter of time until proper legislation would do away with the abuses of lay trusteeism. Meanwhile, the existing Board of Trustees at the cathedral, seeing in the Hughes preamble and resolutions an indictment of their motives and conduct, voted unanimously against their adoption. However, in the elections of 1840, a more tractable board of trustees reversed the decision of their predecessors by voting favorably on the Hughes preamble and resolutions which were adopted *in toto* at their June 24, 1840 meeting.[52]

The prominent role of Hughes in the trustee controversy in New York is accounted for by the fact that shortly after his consecration in St. Patrick's Cathedral by Bishop Dubois, the latter suffered a stroke from which he never recovered. Even before he was named administrator in August 1839, Hughes had assumed responsibility for directing affairs in the diocese to which he would succeed following the death of Dubois in December 1842.[53] Although New York was destined to become the metropolis of the new world, at this time the upper reach of the city was only present-day 14th Street. Nevertheless, a perceptive writer of the time, describing the New York of 1839, forecast its future as follows:

The principal business of our goodly city...seems to

be to unmake what has cost years of labour and heaps of money in the erection. Never was the organ of destructiveness more prominently developed among any people than among the New Yorkers. No sooner has a splendid pile of buildings been erected...than a new whim arises, the work of demolition commences and another "castle in the air" is made to take its place, but fated, like the former, to be prostrated by...the hand of destruction, under the semblance of improvement, leaving a large number of buildings in ruins. They had cost immense sums...but had stood so long (perhaps about five whole years) that they had become antiquated and disagreeable to the modern taste of the new race who had come upon the stage within a year or two past.[54]

A sharp contrast to the above is offered by the penury of the diocese which, at this time and for eight years thereafter,[55] comprised all of New York State and the northern part of New Jersey. Thanks to a "memoir" written by Hughes to his agent in Rome, the Reverend Bernard Smith, O.S.B., we have a description of conditions in the diocese between 1838-1858.[56] Through Smith, this lengthy report on affairs in New York covering a period of twenty years was intended to reach the officials of the Congregation of the Propaganda to counteract statements in the New York *Times* casting "odium and contempt" on Hughes for, among other things, "not having built more and better churches, and not having educated a more numerous, and a more learned clergy."

In 1838 the diocese comprised an extent of territory "larger than all England," with but forty-six churches and as many priests for the scattered Catholic population. In contrast, by 1858 New York City alone had twenty-five churches (including four German churches) and six large chapels attached to as many religious communities, with sixty priests and a Catholic population estimated at between

200,000 and 250,000. Moreover, numerous charitable and educational institutions had been established, including a House of Mercy in 1841 for "destitute females of good character," St. Vincent's Hospital at 11th and 12th Streets in 1849, and a male orphan asylum, built at Fifty-first Street on ground donated by the Common Council in 1846. By 1857, the number of children in Catholic free schools totaled 10,900 and were taught by some 138 teachers, while higher schools for females accounted for another 708 students and 84 teachers, and colleges and higher schools for males an additional 530 with 48 teachers. When the 800 in orphan asylums and their 46 teachers were added, the total enrollment was 12,938 pupils and 316 teachers in New York educational institutions under Catholic auspices. As Hughes pointed out, all of the above were supported by the free offerings of the Catholic people of the city. St. John's College and Seminary had been established at Fordham in 1841 and 1844 respectively, and from the latter the diocese was provided with four or five priests annually .[57]

The Hughes "memoir" also contained an account of the problem of trusteeism which divided the government of the Church between the authority of the bishop and that of lay trustees acting under the authority of the State and controlling the revenues of the congregations.[58] Noting that his two predecessors in New York had, "through necessity," submitted to this system and that "the laity had . . . become accustomed to regard this. . . division of Church authority. . . as a matter of course," Hughes described how he had "made war on the whole system." The result was that "in a very short time. . . the trustees of the churches in this city and in the Diocese. . . became docile and respectful towards Episcopal authority, and. . . the whole system was overthrown, within a period of two or three years. . ."[59] Among the other evils threatening his flock during this period, Hughes included the "Red Republicanism" of Europe with its spurious definition of "Liberty, the progress of human freedom...etc., etc." that attracted so many "blind idolators" in the United States, including many Catholics of New York.[60] The enthusiasm of the latter was considerably shaken, however, when the news that Pius IX had been driven from Rome reached the United States, causing great rejoicing among non-Catholic Americans.[61]

Closer to home and even more menacing was the growing hostility of American Protestants to the increasing number of Catholics in the country. This animus against those of the Catholic faith had been brought to America in 1607 with the founding of Jamestown and would continue long after American independence and the establishment of the new republic. In the 1850's it found expression in the political activity of the American or Know-Nothing Party, a secret association made up of the enemies of the Catholic Church who were bound by oath to make no revelation of its secrets, even in courts of justice. In his report, Hughes rejected the pretense that the Know-Nothing hostility was not so much against Catholics as against foreigners, pointing out that "at the present time whenever the Church is more represented by Native American Catholics, than by foreigners, there she is most oppressed and persecuted." Even as he wrote, Hughes added, "the Cities of Baltimore, of New Orleans, and of Louisville, are, at the present moment, under a 'reign of terror,' and these are, of all others, the cities that are most numerously represented by Catholics born on the soil."[62] In the closing remarks of this "memoir," Hughes made reference to a work he had published in 1856 entitled "Reflections and Suggestions in Regard to What is Called the Catholic Press in the United States." Among the suggestions offered by the archbishop to the editors of such publications was that they "abstain from everything having even a tendency to infringe on the regular ecclesiastical authority ...that...Catholic doctrine and the politics of the country be not blended together in the same columns;...and, finally, that no Catholic newspaper should attempt, whether intentionally or not, to sow discord among them," i.e. the Catholics of New York.[63] This lengthy document, curiously enough, contained no mention of the projected new cathedral, the cornerstone of which Hughes would bless approximately two months after the date of his "memoir."

During the early decades of the history of antebellum New York, as Catholicism there was developing in a predominantly Protestant society, the city itself was undergoing dramatic changes. Following the British evacuation of New York in November 1783, a program of building and renovation was inaugurated to replace the devastation wrought by the years of war and occupation. Families returning to the city found their homes and gardens plundered, their churches left empty shells after being used as hospitals, prisons, etc., while warehouses and stores were stripped of their contents and wharves and docks were all but ruined and streets were rutted and dirty. As the properties of the Loyalists, many of whom had earlier departed for Canada, the West Indies or England, were sold to the returning patriots, a busy period of restoration followed. Despite such problems, the city enjoyed a certain excitement and pageantry during these early years, serving as it did as the state capital (1784-97) and, more briefly (1785-90) as the temporary meeting place of the federal government. When, on April 30, 1789, President George Washington took the oath of office on the balcony of Federal Hall in Wall Street, an immense crowd of spectators jammed the surrounding sidewalks, streets, windows and even roof tops. However, with the transfer of the federal capital to Philadelphia in August 1790, Congress and the Washingtons moved to that city where they remained until 1800 when the permanent seat of government in Washington, D.C., was ready to receive them. Three years earlier, Albany had become the permanent state capital of New York.

The economic situation of the city greatly improved as the Far Eastern trade, originated with the first voyage of the *Empress of China* in 1784, proved so profitable that a thriving China trade developed. Since the location of the port of New York offered an excellent exchange center, cargoes from other states were delivered there for transshipment across the Atlantic, while goods coming from Europe to New York were then distributed to other American cities. In one year (1788) more than 1,000 ships entered the harbor and nearly $2,000,000 worth of products were transported out through the port of New York. As the increase of commerce and wealth drew more people to New York, the city's population, which had dropped to about 10,000 in 1783, rose to 23,614 by 1787, exceeding the prewar figure. By 1820, residents of the city numbered 123,700, many of whom had come from other states and an increasing number from France, Ireland and Germany. Despite outbreaks of yellow fever in 1822 and 1823, bringing death to hundreds of its victims daily, the city's population rose to 202,589 by 1830 and reached 312,710 ten years later.[64]

In 1825, the opening of the Erie Canal, uniting Lake Erie with the Hudson River, further stimulated business in the city as within a year an estimated five hundred new mercantile houses, twelve banks and ten marine insurance companies opened their doors, while charters for twenty-seven more banks awaited approval by the Legislature. By this time the city had fifty newspapers which were hawked by young boys through the streets. A few years later, the first railroad on Manhattan Island was incorporated (April 25, 1831) as the New York and Harlem Company and authorized to build a single or double track north of 23rd Street anywhere between Third and Eighth Avenues to any point on the Harlem River. Following the Great Fire of 1835 which burned over seventeen blocks, more than six hundred buildings east of Broadway and south of Wall Street were wiped out together with what was left of the old Dutch city. The rebuilding effort started a boom not only in the burned out tract, but in other areas as well. Many private houses on Broadway were abandoned to trade as those whose places had been destroyed moved there, and their former owners located on side streets as far as 23rd Street on the edge of open country. Vast numbers of manual laborers were required for all these building efforts and many immigrants who were recruited for these jobs did their work well.[65]

As the city prospered, trends in the distribution of the city's wealth showed a degree of inequality that worsened with the passage of time. In 1828, one percent of the city's adults owned about forty percent of the city's wealth, while the next richest three percent of wealthy adults held an additional twenty percent. By 1845, the richest one percent owned about half the wealth, with the richest four percent worth more than eighty percent of the total. Thus only a small percentage was shared with the mass of the city's population, made up of laborers, artisans, clerks and petty shopkeepers, bearing out the statement of Philip Hone that the city at midcentury had "arrived at the state of society to be found in the large cities of Europe," in which "the two extremes of costly luxury in living, expensive establishments and improvident waste are presented in daily and hourly contrast with squalid misery and hopeless destitution."[66]

CHAPTER II

A Cathedral of Suitable Magnificence

John Hughes was not a man to limit himself to small dreams, nor to delay in translating them into reality. Even the heightening in the 1850's of the traditional anti-Catholic bigotry, built on the nativists' violent hatred of Irish Catholicism and immigants in general, did not deter him from proceeding with his plans for a "cathedral of suitable magnificence for the Church of New York." In 1853, the same year Hughes chose James Renwick as the architect for his cathedral, vicious fighting beween nativist Protestants and Irish Catholics disturbed the peace of the Ninth Ward of the city. There, the long pent-up hostilities released on July 4 were subdued only when the National Guard arrived and succeeded in finally quelling the rioting. Some five months later, a large demonstration was staged in the park, mostly in criticism of Mayor Jacob Westervelt for the arrest of an anti-Catholic agitator who, while rabble-rousing during a street demonstration, had verbally attacked Hughes, the "Pope of New York," and Catholics as "threats to American freedom and morality and an ever present danger to American independence."[1]

Other developments in the city during these years likewise served to remind New Yorkers that deep-rooted problems remained to be solved. In 1855 New York City's population had reached 629,904 (almost double that of 1845), more than half of whom were immigrants, including 175,737 Irish and 95,572 Germans, the latter growing at a greater rate than the Irish. Even more disturbing to the nativists was the fact that while the more than 300,000 newcomers arriving in 1854 constituted half of the city's population, they made up seventy-five per cent of the inmates of the almhouses, work-houses, the city prisons and the state penitentiary. To add to the city's woes, the financial panic in early fall of 1857 threatened more social unrest as hundreds of businesses failed, banks closed and tens of thousands lost their jobs. Street demonstrations in the city by the Irish featured signs calling for "Work" and those by the Germans demanded "Arbeit."[2] Fortunately, legislation in response to reformers' demands for "a great park to act as lungs for the city" had been passed earlier in 1857. Faced by the threat of mob violence, the city council appropriated $250,000 for the project, thus providing thousands with work on its roads, lakes and structures.[3]

If there were no easy solutions to the city's problems of poverty and crime, or for the frequent outbursts of street violence they spawned, the same was also true of the greater issues facing the country at large. By mid-century, mer-chants of the city had built up a brisk trade with the south, the former selling cotton for southern plantation owners who, in turn, purchased furniture and household goods from the city. Many New Yorkers were friends of south-erners, and numbers of the latter often visited the city during the summer and sent their children to New York schools. Indeed, in some ways the metropolis was not unlike a south-ern community, for Blacks in the city attended separate "colored schools," and theaters, churches and public trans-portation were segregated. Constituting only about one per cent of the population, some 12,000 in all, Blacks had little political power. Moreover, their situation worsened each year as the hundreds of thousands of immigrants arriving at Castle Garden not only added to the city's population, but

Photograph by Mathew Brady

John Hughes, first Archbishop
of New York (1850-1864)

heightened the competition for jobs, housing and a better life, intensifying racial tensions and deepening social antagonisms.[4] As New Yorkers began to realize the seriousness of the questions of slavery and states' rights and their threat to national union, their views were debated in the streets as well as in the newspapers.

Despite these threatening and ominous times, Hughes never faltered in his determination "to erect a cathedral in the city of New York that may be worthy of our increasing numbers, intelligence, and wealth as a religious community, and...as a public architectural monument of the present and prospective greatness of this metropolis of the American Continent."[5] There was no question in his mind as to the proper site for the cathedral, for he had earlier determined upon using property located on the Middle Road, later known as Fifth Avenue, between Fiftieth and Fifty-first Streets.[6] In 1828 this site had been purchased jointly by the trustees of St. Patrick's Cathedral and St. Peter's Church, as equal owners, for use as a burial ground at a cost of $5,500.[7] But the nature of the land, almost solid rock, and its location so far beyond city limits made its use as a cemetery impractical. Thus in 1832, a plot at 11th and 12th Streets between Avenue A and First Avenue was secured and served as a burial place until Calvary Cemetery was opened in 1848.[8] The cathedral trustees became the sole owner of the Fifth Avenue property when, in 1852, they purchased at auction the thirty-eight lots formerly held by the trustees of St. Peter's Church.[9] The latter had become virtually bankrupt in 1844, with claims against them amounting to almost $140,000 by 1849; thus the $59,575 paid to St. Peter's for the Fifth Avenue property helped to ease the financial pressure on that parish.[10] In order to raise that amount, the cathedral trustees had been obliged to mortgage "the entire Block comprised between 50th and 51st Streets and 4th and 5th Avenues, and also the lots belonging to this corporation fronting on 1st Avenue between 11th and 12th Streets as security for the said loan of $50,000." In addition, the cathedral trustees called upon the Sisters of Charity of Mount Saint Vincent for the sum of $11,000 "heretofore advanced to them by this corporation."[11]

The location chosen by Hughes for his new cathedral was not an unfamiliar sight to the many native New Yorkers and visitors to the city who, all during the 1850's, summer and winter, enjoyed the drive out of town to the upper reaches of Manhattan. Croton Reservoir, then located on the west side of Fifth Avenue between 40th and 42nd Streets, was a favorite destination. From the promenade atop its walls visitors could enjoy a fine view of the city to the south, as well as of the Hudson and East Rivers, and to the northwest the villages of Yorkville, Manhattanville and Harlem.[12] In 1853, an area behind the reservoir was the site for the first World's Fair to be held in the United States, an event that on opening day, July 14, featured a host of visiting dignitaries, including President Franklin Pierce and many members of Congress who were welcomed by Mayor Jacob Westervelt. Addressing the huge crowd assembled to welcome him, Pierce offered his congratulations to the citizens of the Empire City for building in only a few years one of the most important cities of the world.[13] Soon after this event, many curious New Yorkers were driving farther north on Fifth Avenue to see the site chosen by Hughes for New York's new cathedral which some would ridicule, calling it "Hughes' folly ."[14]

It was sometime during 1853 that Hughes opened discussions with James Renwick, Jr., an Episcopalian, the son of a Columbia College professor and himself a Columbia College graduate at the age of nineteen.[15] While serving as assistant engineer of the Croton water system, Renwick had supervised the construction of the reservoir on the 42nd Street site (later Bryant Park), a project that took five years and cost twelve and a half million dollars.[16] His architectural career began in 1843 when his plans won the competition for Grace Episcopal Church in New York, the construction of which was completed in 1846. During the early stages of planning the new St. Patrick's, Renwick had the assistance of William Rodrigue, who in the early 1800's had designed Hughes' Church of St. John in Philadelphia, and who later (1836) married Hughes' sister Margaret.[17] Although the cathedral archives contain several drawings which bear the signatures of both Renwick and Rodrigue, it is the judgment of the present architect of the cathedral, Walter Knight Sturges, that "When we examine Renwick's final design, signed and dated April 1867. . . it is very clear that the 1858 design has been pulled together by the hand of a master, and this drawing carries Renwick's signature alone."[18] Thanks to his genius, the design of St. Patrick's as executed would provide New York with one of the outstanding examples of the Gothic Revival.

As the plans for the new St. Patrick's approached completion, Hughes wrote to the cathedral trustees stating "I do not wish the Board of the Cathedral to be a party to any of the contracts for the erection of the new St. Patrick's, except perhaps as individuals, but not as a Board." However, he suggested that in their corporate capacity they might pay for the grading of the cathedral site and also purchase in their own name some eight or nine acres containing the quarry from which the stone for the new building was to be taken. He pointed out that by owning this, "it will render us independent of the caprices of quarry owners and quarry men." Moreover, "by laying a railway for a short distance, the car can be loaded in the quarry itself, and by another railway. . . the same cars can be unloaded around the new building." In carrying out the cathedral project, Hughes was determined "to pay as we go so far as materials and workmen are concerned" but, as he pointed out, this would be

*James Renwick, Jr. and his rendering
of the Cathedral, 1858*

possible only if the necessary contributions were received.[19]

Some days later, on July 14, 1858, the archbishop addressed a circular letter to about 140 Catholics in the city and Diocese of New York, sending copies also to "two or three...prominent Catholics out of the diocese."[20] In the circular, Hughes first announced his intention to call in person at the earliest opportunity in reference to the new cathedral to be erected on Fifth Avenue. Declaring that the ultimate success of this undertaking was not doubtful, he emphasized that "its triumphal accomplishment will depend in a great measure on the responses which I am to receive from those to whom I have the honor of addressing this letter." The only object of the latter was "to ascertain whether there are not in my Diocese, or rather in the city of New York itself, one hundred persons who will subscribe $1,000 each..."[21] If desired, these could be paid in quarterly installments during the first year, to be used "expressly and exclusively...to carry on the work during the same period." Anticipating that it would take five years to complete the work, Hughes declared "Everything depends on the first year. My principle is to pay as we proceed, up to an amount of half a million dollars; and if at that point it should be necessary to obtain a loan of two or three hundred thousand dollars, I do not think that this need frighten any one."[22]

John Hughes himself had great confidence in the success of his undertaking which he believed to be "for the glory of God, for the exaltation of our Holy Mother Church, the honor of the Catholic name in this country, and as a monument of which the city of New York either in its present or prospective greatness need never be ashamed." A month before launching his appeal for funds, he had advised the cathedral trustees that he would lay the corner stone "please God, on Sunday, the 15th of August at 4 o'clock in the afternoon," adding "if I should not live to see the work completed, others will, and in order that they may, I must begin."[23] These sentiments were echoed in the archbishop's circular letter in which he stated that even if his appeal for funds proved unsuccessful, "the corner-stone shall be laid the same and protected by an iron railing against possible injury until the arrival of better times." Knowing that he would never have the consolation of seeing his cathedral consecrated, Hughes was determined that the honor and privilege of beginning it would not be left to his successor.[24]

During the summer of 1858, Hughes wrote frequently to his friend and agent in Rome, Father Bernard Smith, O.S.B., describing how busy he was with the preparations for the great event of August 15. "All the Bishops of this Province have most kindly consented to give solemnity to the occasion by their presence" he wrote, and "one hundred and twenty boys [are] in preparation for responding to the choir and the clergy in chanting the appropriate Psalms." By August 12, the archbishop could report to his Roman friend that although "I have not been more than twenty hours altogether in making these visits to collect money for the new Cathedral...more than one hundred have given one thousand dollars each for the first year..." Hughes' prediction that the August 15th ceremony "on the scale which I have projected it will produce a sensation" proved to be very close to the mark. An immense audience of some 100,000 persons presented themselves at the 50th Street site on the afternoon of August 15, the more affluent having arrived by carriage, while the more numerous thousands had taxed to capacity, and beyond, the services afforded by the five railroad lines then serving the city. Although a substantial majority of the spectators were Catholics, their numbers were increased by "a very large number of Protestants."[25]

In his address, Hughes first thanked the visiting prelates, his own clergy and those present as representatives of other jurisdictions for the honor of their presence. To the members of his own flock "who, in the main, constitute the vast assemblage of persons," he felt no expression of gratitude was necessary because "that they know already — for...if they had not responded in such numbers as they have done, it would be the first time that they have failed me. This they have never done, this...they will never do...."[26] Then, referring to his circular letter of June 14th, he announced that his "bold expectations have been realized; that I have found one hundred persons who have subscribed, and many of them already paid, $1000 each...to carry on this great work during the first year of its progress...." These first patrons of the projected cathedral, among whom were two non-Catholics,[27] included representatives of the United States, Ireland, Scotland, England, Belgium, Spain, France and Germany. Their names, engrossed on a parchment scroll, were placed in the cavity of the cornerstone laid that day.[28] In reporting this eventful occasion, the *Times* called it "memorable," adding "there was no exception to the general satisfaction."[29]

The ensuing months found Hughes busily engaged in working out the contractual arrangements with the architects and builders, selecting the materials to be used and estimating costs. The terms of the contract with Messers. James Renwick, Jr., and William Rodrigue, dated March 5, 1859, provided that the architects were to receive $2,500 a year for eight years, reserving to the archbishop the right to suspend or discontinue the building at any time. After examining four varieties of stone, the most expensive, white marble, was chosen for its beauty and durability which more than justified the additional expense. Messrs. James Hall and William Joyce of the East Chester Quarry, having estimated that the cost of building the whole cathedral of white marble would amount to $850,000, signed a contract on March 5, 1859, for the construction of the entire work except the altars and furnishings. The contract also included a clause binding "the parties of the second part" to ban "any spirituous liquors" from being brought or used on the construction site and to "instantly discharge any workman who may bring or use the same thereon." Furthermore, no workman could be employed who lived or boarded at any place in which spirituous liquors were sold "within two blocks east or west, or four blocks north or south of said premises, under pain of forfeiture of this contract."[30] In this connection, it is interesting to note that at the time it was estimated that of the 5,980 taverns and 2,000 beer parlors in the city, "one-half to two-thirds of all groggeries are owned by Catholics." Moreover, Catholics were said to "sell much more than their proportion of the liquor drunk in this country."[31] A widely held assumption that Irish Catholics also consumed "more than their proportion" of the liquor sold in the city was greatly reenforced by the revitalized nativism of the 1850's, and later perpetuated by the caricaturist art of Thomas Nast of *Harper's Weekly.*[32]

Work on the new cathedral was soon initiated and the rapid progress made during the next two years saw the completion of the foundation and construction up to the water table. By then, all the funds collected, $73,000,[33] had been expended, so Hughes decided to discontinue the work until more money could be raised. Meanwhile, the threat of civil war had grown ever more certain, but even as New Yorkers worried about the future, they welcomed the distractions offered by the visits to their city of a number of foreign dignitaries. The seventeen-year-old, four-foot-high Crown Prince Tateish Onojero of Japan, arriving in the city in June 1860 with his entourage, generated a high degree of excitement among the vast crowds who watched the procession from the Battery up Broadway to the park. That fall, the Prince of Wales, son of Queen Victoria and later King Edward VII, arrived at Castle Garden for a visit that was cited as an example of the "Entente Cordiale" with England.

Among the many flags decorating the Garden, the largest banner was the huge green one with the Hibernian harp in the center! At the dinner hosted by Mayor Fernando Wood, the honored guests included Archbishop John Hughes and Charles O'Conor, as well as John Jacob and William B. Astor and other prominent New Yorkers.[34]

Two months later in December, South Carolina, followed by other southern states, dissolved their ties with the Union and the new political unit, the Confederate States of America, was established. The effect in New York of this development was to make the city zealously patriotic. When Abraham Lincoln visited New York on February 19, 1861, the reception he received and the warm expressions of loyalty were in sharp contrast to the lack of attention that had marked his previous visit the year before when he had delivered an address at Cooper Union.[35] Some months later, in October, the services of the Archbishop of New York were sought by the United States government when President Lincoln and Secretary of State William H. Seward, asked Hughes to visit Europe in an effort to gain support for the Union cause. In accepting the commission, Hughes considered it to be "in harmony with my personal character—still more with my ecclesiastical character."[36] Although Hughes had small success in England, he wrote to Seward from Paris to report that Napoleon III's speech on January 27, 1862, to the legislative assembly was all that "under present circumstances, we could have hoped for...I regard it as a proclamation of peace on the part of France, from which England may take a lesson of wisdom..."[37]

As the war dragged on and problems multiplied, some New Yorkers began to call for "peace and conciliation." But it was the decision to institute conscription that brought the angriest cries of all. During the first week of July 1863, rumors abounded in the city regarding armed resistance to the draft, a piece of legislation which was especially objectionable because it allowed the wealthy to pay $300 to buy a substitute. When the drawing for the draft was first instituted on Saturday, July 11, nothing untoward occurred. However, Sunday's leisure time provided an opportunity for heated discussions which, with heavy consumption of alcoholic beverages, inevitably led to the outbreak of violence that occurred the following morning when the draft office opened. After setting fire to the lottery wheel and destroying the building in which it was housed, an ugly mob ran wildly through the city streets committing other atrocities.[38]

Hughes, who had returned from Europe a sick man, was now called upon by New York's Governor Horatio Seymour to stop the disorders rampant in the city. Physically unable to go to the rioters, the archbishop had an invitation posted around the city asking the men to come to him. In response, some three or four thousand gathered around his residence at the northwest corner of 36th Street and Madison Avenue where, seated in a chair on the balcony of his home, Hughes spoke to them. Appealing to the rioters "to respect the laws of man and the peace of society," he urged them "to retire to their homes with as little delay as possible, and to disconnect themselves from the seemingly deliberate intention to disturb the peace and social rights of the citizens of New York." In his weakened condition, Hughes' voice was barely audible to the large gathering, but after listening intently the men quietly dispersed.[39]

The occasion marked Hughes' last public appearance. His conditioned worsened and he lingered on for some months, slipping away peacefully on January 3, 1864, while Albany's Bishop John McCloskey was reciting the prayers of the Church for the dying.[40] In the cathedral on Mott Street, the archbishop's body, resting on a catafalque, was placed on the very spot where he had knelt twenty-six years earlier to receive episcopal consecration. On January 7th,

the anniversary of his consecration, the mortal remains of
the first Archbishop of New York were laid to rest in the
vault of the old cathedral, to be transferred some nineteen
years later to the crypt of the noble edifice on Fifth Avenue
which his foresight and courage had initiated.[41]

The first native of New York State to enter the diocesan
priesthood, John McCloskey had been ordained by Bishop
Dubois in 1834 and then served for a short time as vice
president and professor of philosophy in the seminary at
Nyack. When the latter burned down, he was sent to Rome
where he spent the next three years as a student at the
Roman College, later the Gregorian University. Returning
to New York in 1837, he was appointed rector of St.
Joseph's Church and also served for a time as first president
of St. John's College. Following his consecration on March
10, 1844, as titular Bishop of Axiere and coadjutor with
right of succession to Hughes, he assisted the latter by
making episcopal visitations and serving in various other
capacities. When, on April 23, 1847, Albany was erected
into a separate diocese, McCloskey was transferred there
and installed by Bishop Hughes on September 19, 1847,
serving that diocese for seventeen years until his return to
New York as the successor to Hughes. Installed in New
York on August 21, 1864, the gentle McCloskey provided a
striking contrast to the vigorous and unyielding Hughes.
Nevertheless, the former proved eminently successful in
administering the affairs of his vast archdiocese and was
destined to be the first American to become a member of the
College of Cardinals, an honor President Lincoln had not
succeeded in obtaining for John Hughes.[42]

When, as early as 1864, there were rumors of the possibility of the creation of an American cardinal, McCloskey's
views on the subject were set forth in a letter to Archbishop
Martin J. Spalding of Baltimore. "Is it not provoking," he
wrote, "to have to endure such ridiculous reports...I hope

John Cardinal McCloskey
Archbishop of New York (1864-1885)

we shall have no cardinal's hat in this country. We are better
without one." Many Catholics of the time shared the
archbishop's sentiments, fearing that an appointment of this
kind would surely be the signal for an outburst of bigotry
and intolerance. A decade later, however, some of the
sharpness of the earlier prejudice had disappeared, so that
when the news arrived that Pius IX had precognized John
McCloskey in the public consistory of March 15, 1875, there
was almost universal approval in the United States. In
accepting the cardinalatial honor, McCloskey did so as a
distinction conferred upon the Church in America, stating
"Not to my poor merits, but to those of the young and
already vigorous and...flourishing Catholic Church of
America has this honor been given...." He also made it
clear that when the Pope decided to confer such an honor,
"he had regard to the dignity of the See of New York, to the
merits and devotion of the venerable clergy and numerous
laity, and...even the eminent rank of this great city and the
glorious American nation."

Meanwhile, McCloskey had lost no time in carrying forward the work on the cathedral begun by his predecessor.
As early as May 1865, he had written to Archbishop Spalding that to his other burdens was added "the delectable one
of begging for the new Cathedral," "a work which he
claimed took every leisure moment and a great deal more."[43] In
a circular letter, dated March 17, 1865, the archbishop had
announced his plans to resume work on the cathedral at as
early a date as possible, adding that before that could be
done it was neessary to "resume...the work of *collecting*."
He then urged all the subscribers to Hughes' first appeal
who had not yet "fully complied with their engage-
ment...to make good the balance..." All others who
could afford to give $1000 were also invited to do so and
thus "rank among the first Patrons and largest Benefactors
of the New Cathedral." When the first appeal was made, it

St. Patrick's in 1868

was intended that, "in due time it would be succeeded by a second, comprising those who . . . would contribute a sum of not less than Five Hundred Dollars." Estimating that there must be at least two hundred "to whom God has given the means, and whom He will inspire with the zeal and generosity to contribute the amount named," he urged all to fulfil their commitments within five or six months after May 1, 1865.[44]

Collecting for the new cathedral did not long remain a "delectable" task for McCloskey to whom, by the following October, it had become "unpleasant work."[45] However, it would appear that committees appointed by the archbishop to solicit individual subscriptions enjoyed considerable success if the report of one committee for the 7th District was at all typical. During the two months of February and March 1871, this committee reported subscriptions totaling $111,150, of which two were over $5000, five of $5000, forty-two of $1000, forty-six of $500, twenty-nine of $250, and twenty-four in the amount of $100.[46] One of the two who contributed over $5000 was William Shakespeare Caldwell, wealthy layman of New York and father of Mary Gwendolyn (Mamie) Caldwell, who was instrumental in launching The Catholic University of America with her large donation of $300,000.[47] Over the years, assessments on the parishes of the archdiocese brought in substantial sums, the result of not inconsiderable sacrifice on the part of pastors and parishioners.[48]

Because the struggle to keep ahead of the costs of construction was an unrelenting one, McCloskey on occasion sought the aid of his lay board of trustees. In 1866, for example, the latter responded by voting to sell eight lots of land on 11th and 12th Streets owned by the Corporation of St. Patrick's and to apply the proceeds towards the erection of the Fifth Avenue cathedral. Again, in 1873, the trustees raised money by applying for a "Bond and Mortage on the Archbishop's residence and premises for $40,000, the proceeds of such...to be applied towards the erection of the new Cathedral." The trustees also obtained loans of $300,000 in 1874 and an additional $100,000 in 1876 from the Emigrant Industrial Savings Bank of the City of New York, secured by mortgage on the "property of this Corporation situated on Fifth Avenue and 50th-51st Streets in the City of New York."[49] The crowning fund-raising event, the so-called "Cathedral Fair," was held in the completed interior of the new cathedral from October 22 to November 30, 1878. Receipts from that effort which included the sale of a daily publication, *Journal of the Fair*, amounted to a grand total of $172,625.48,[50] a sum which helped to hasten the day of the formal opening and blessing of the new St. Patrick's.

That historic event occurred on May 25, 1879, the feast of St. Gregory VII, receiving unprecedented publicity and attesting to the improvement in public sentiment towards the Church, at least for the time. New Yorkers, Catholic and non-Catholic alike, shared a sense of pride that their city was now graced by such a magnificent Gothic structure, the first of its kind in the United States.[51] Archbishop Hughes had earlier determined that the special patron of the cathedral was to be "the glorious apostle of Ireland—St. Patrick." Fears concerning this choice were expressed in a letter to Cardinal McCloskey from "A Catholic American," who believed that the name would be "prejudicial to the cause of Catholicity among the Protestant portion of Americans ...and looked upon as so very un-American and simply a piece of Irish egotism."[52] Happily, this prophecy proved unfounded when many of the newspapers of the day hailed the new St. Patrick's Cathedral as "the noblest temple ever raised to the memory of St. Patrick." Its granite and marble exterior was likened to that of the Cologne cathedral, while the interior was said to resemble the cathedral of Amiens, "a forest of white marble piers, kaleidoscopic stained-glass windows, dominated by an impressive rose window twenty-six feet in diameter."[53] The *American Architect and Building News* declared "The Roman Catholic Church is the only body which would have dared attempt such a structure among us."[54]

The solemn rite of blessing and dedication was performed by Cardinal McCloskey, attended by six archbishops, thirty-five bishops and more than four hundred priests,[55] in the presence of a congregation which the New York *Times* declared "couldn't have been less than seven thousand persons."[56] Bishop Patrick John Ryan, then coadjutor of St. Louis, Missouri, and the outstanding ecclesiastical orator of his time, delivered the sermon for this occasion as he would for a number of important future events in the history of the cathedral.[57] In addressing those crowded in the cathedral, Ryan called St. Patrick's a "splendid refutation" of the charge that the utilitarian nineteenth century was incapable of producing cathedrals like those of past ages "because the faith that built them was dying or dead." Bidding all present to rejoice that evidence of the spirit of the ages of faith "lives on in the majesty of St. Patrick's," the preacher commended "the rich Catholics of this metropolis;" the "children of toil," who gave generously of their scanty means; and the "liberal non-Catholics of New York" who helped in the great work. As the "greatest church edifice of the New World, the ornament of their city, the temple of religious art," Ryan also saw the cathedral as "the powerful means of preserving morality amongst those who shall worship within its walls."[58] With its dedication, the Fifth Avenue St. Patrick's became the cathedral church of the archdiocese, while the old cathedral, thereafter known as St. Patrick's Church, continued to minister to the Catholics of lower Manhattan. Under the chairmanship of the successive ordinaries of New York, a single legal entity, incorporated in 1817 as "The Trustees of St. Patrick's Cathedral in the City of New York," consisting of laymen, has served in an advisory capacity in the management of the temporal affairs of the two St. Patrick's and the several cemeteries of the archdiocese.

In the Gothic tradition of the Continent, Renwick, in his early plans, had included an apsidal chapel for the cathedral, but Hughes had requested a modification of this plan in order to reduce costs.[59] Thus, the building as dedicated in 1879 terminated abruptly behind the high altar and remained that way for more than twenty years. In 1899, when Archbishop Michael A. Corrigan was left a bequest of $200,000 in the will of Mrs. Eugene Kelly[60] "for the purpose of completing the Cathedral by the erection of the Lady Chapel," he turned this money over to the cathedral trustees for the purpose of the legacy.[61] By spring 1900, the plans submitted by Charles T. Matthews, one of the fifteen leading Gothic architects of New York who had engaged in the architectural competition, were approved by Mrs. Kelly's sons, Eugene and Thomas H. Kelly. However, the legacy proved inadequate to carry out "the exquisite and elaborate details contained in the accepted plans." When the possibility of raising additional funds was considered, Eugene and Thomas H. Kelly informed the trustees that they would donate, not later than January 1, 1904, the additional amount required ($165,000) for the construction of the Lady Chapel proper.

Although the architect chosen possessed unusual artistic knowledge and ability, he lacked the engineering experience necessary for the work, so a general contractor, Mr. Charles T. Wills, was engaged in June 1901.[62] It was agreed that the cathedral trustees would assume the expenses for the work of excavating the sub-cellars and basement of the Lady Chapel to provide a "suitable Sacristy[63]...and...a proper approach by a stairway from the said Sacristy to the Chapel." The trustees were also to be responsible for the costs involved in providing passageways between the cathedral and the episcopal residence on the 50th Street side, and the cathedral and the rectory on the 51st Street side of the cathedral.[64] A number of other adjustments were made as the work progressed, but the Lady Chapel was finally completed in time for the first Mass to be offered there on Christmas 1906. With the removal of the east wall of the original structure, the side aisles were continued as an ambulatory leading back of the high altar and into the Lady Chapel, which was flanked by two small semi-octagonal chapels. The effect of these changes, which added 296 square yards of space to the cathedral,[65] was to provide a very pleasing vista which, from the west portal, made the building appear half again as long as its former length.

Work on the spires, which in 1879 reached only to the level of the roof, was initiated in the fall of 1885 and completed in early October 1888. The cost was estimated at $200,000, of which $120,000 had been contributed by the faithful. The estimated cost of the building, before the spires were added, was $1,900,000. Renwick believed the total cost

was between $2,000,000 and $2,500,000, with the latter figure probably the more correct one. By the early 1900's, the
cost had reached about $4,000,000[66] and it continued to rise
through the decades that followed as additional improvements were planned and executed. An extensive interior
renovation of the cathedral to comply with strict liturgical
requirements and to satisfy the building's architectural
implications was initiated by Cardinal Patrick J. Hayes and
completed by his successor, Francis Spellman, part of the
cost of which was drawn from the $3,000,000 Major Bowes
Fund left to the cathedral by the author of the famous
amateur radio program.[67]

During the twenty-one years that separated the laying of
the cornerstone and the dedication of the new St. Patrick's,
the growth of both trade and population confirmed the
diverse character of New York society that has remained
one of its distinguishing marks to the present day. By 1870,
there were more than 400,000 foreign-born in the city, well
over forty-four percent of its inhabitants, forming a large,
resourceless and poor element of the population. Most
numerous were the Irish and the Germans, comprising
twenty-eight and fifteen percent, respectively, of the total
residents.[68] One consequence of this growth in population
was to force settlement to move rapidly northward so that
by 1860 the built-up area had reached 42nd Street and
would soon spread to the fifties. The German "Dutch Hill"
near the East River between 38th and 44th Streets matched
the Irish shanty towns a little farther north near the Hudson
River. When the latter were pointed out to the future
Charles Lord Russell of Killowen as he steamed up the
Hudson during his visit to this country in 1883, he found the
scene "a melancholy and indeed a humiliating one to an
Irishman," regarding the wretched structures as "abodes
...which a well-bred dog would scorn."[69]

A drive along Fifth Avenue took Russell past the new St.

Patrick's which, he noted, "is *the* church of New York, as far as architectural beauty and grandeur are concerned." He and his companion, however, were surprised by "the smallness of the Catholic congregation. The church was not half-filled." Acknowledging that a possible explanation might be that it was High Mass and that August "is a dull season," he added, "still we thought it remarkable." He found the people of New York "as civil if not as polite as the Parisians in the days of the Empire, and certainly much more civil than the general run of Englishmen." He also remarked on the deference paid to women in the railways and stage cars, and the freedom with which they went about alone in the public streets and public conveyances "in a way quite unknown to us." The candor with which men discussed their political, religious and social institutions, and admitted "with great frankness the blots in the existing condition of things," was also striking to Russell. Although at this time he saw that "at present the tide of fashion follows the line of Fifth Avenue," he predicted that "in a few years it will probably be found to contain (at least to a great extent) business houses."[70] Some thirteen years later, Lord Russell returned to the United States to address a meeting of the American Bar Association at Saratoga Springs. Since he kept no diary of this visit, it is not known whether he paid another visit to New York City. Had he done so, he would not have missed the signs that his 1883 prediction about the future of Fifth Avenue appeared to have been well founded.

CHAPTER III

Formative Years

The Rectorships of Monsignor William Quinn,
(1879-87) and Monsignor Michael J. Lavelle,
(1887-1939)

In 1879 the parochial district assigned to the cathedral extended from Seventh Avenue on the west to the East River, and from Forty-sixth Street north to Fifty-ninth Street, with a strip south to Forty-second Street, between Madison and Sixth Avenues.[1] To administer this new parish, Cardinal McCloskey chose the Reverend William Quinn whom he had ordained in 1845 in his capacity as coadjutor to Bishop Hughes. Born in County Donegal, Ireland, on May 21, 1820, Quinn had arrived in New York in 1841 and entered the preparatory seminary of St. John's, Fordham, which had opened the previous June under John McCloskey, who served as president and professor. When in 1842 this double burden proved too great a strain on his health and McCloskey returned to his pastorate at St. Joseph's Church, Quinn was one of the seventeen seminarians of St. John's who expressed sorrow at his departure which, they stated, was only alleviated by their hope that they might "in future intercourse enjoy frequent opportunities of benefitting still further by your learning and piety."[2] Following Quinn's ordination in 1845, he served as assistant at St. Joseph's until September 1849, when he was sent to Rondout as pastor. He was recalled a few months later to administer the troubled affairs at New York's mother church, St. Peter's on Barclay Street, where he remained for

Monsignor William Quinn

twenty-four years. Within his first three years there, Quinn succeeded in carrying out measures to liquidate the large parish debt incurred prior to his appointment, and was congratulated by Archbishop Hughes for his "prudence ...devotion and unceasing energy." Appointed Vicar General of New York in April 1873, Quinn was transferred the following month to the cathedral on Mott Street as pastor.[3]

Because of McCloskey's failing health, responsibility for many of the details regarding the completion of the new cathedral fell to Quinn, who carried out the wishes of the cardinal "with fidelity and skill." At the dedication ceremony on May 25, Quinn, who had been named first rector of the new St. Patrick's, informed his flock that parish life would begin the following Sunday. Since priority had been given to finishing the cathedral, temporary quarters had been provided to house the cardinal and the rector, each with his respective staff members. Cardinal McCloskey and his secretary, Father John Farley, lived at 32 West 56th Street, where they were joined by Michael Corrigan following his appointment on October 1, 1880, as titular Archbishop of Petra and Coadjutor of New York, with the right of succession. When the archiepiscopal residence at 452 Madison Avenue was completed in 1882, the cardinal, his coadjutor and their staff took up residence there. Quinn, who was made a domestic prelate in 1881, lived with his assistants at 26 East 50th Street until the cathedral rectory at 460 Madison Avenue was completed in May 1884.[4]

During the decades between 1880 and World War I, residents of Fifth Avenue and the streets of the Fifties immediately adjacent to it, along with others farther north, represented some of the greatest wealth and financial power in the world. "robber baron" Jay (Jason) Gould in 1880 took up residence in a large house at 579 Fifth Avenue, moving there from a smaller place between 47th and 48th Streets. At his death in 1892, he left $72 million to be divided among his six children. Andrew Carnegie, whose grand mansion on 51st Street, immediately west of Fifth Avenue, had been purchased from Collis Huntington for $170,000 was said to be worth $400 million by 1900. In 1899, work began on the massive palace he ordered built to the north between 91st and 92nd Streets, then practically a wilderness. Retiring in 1901, Carnegie belatedly devoted himself to providing capital for social and educational causes, including the building and equipment of public libraries, the establishment of pension funds for his former employees, and other notable endowments.[5]

William Henry Vanderbilt, infamous for his "the public

be damned" statement, left a family fortune of $200 million at his death in 1885. His three massive brownstones, erected at 640 and 642 Fifth Avenue and 2 West 52nd Street, were so constructed that while normally separate and independent of one another, they could for great occasions be thrown into one. To this brownstone enclave, his son, William Kissam Vanderbilt, added another house at 660 Fifth Avenue on the northwest corner of 52nd Street at a cost of $3 million. Cornelius Vanderbilt and his wife Alice Gwynne Vanderbilt built a gigantic mansion between 57th and 58th Streets on the Avenue, in imitation of William Kissam's home, considered one of the ten best in the United States. Farther north on the Avenue at 858 stood the home of Thomas Fortune Ryan, who served for a time on the Board of Trustees of St. Patrick's Cathedral. This impressive structure contained a private chapel and a valuable collection of medieval and renaissance art. Once a penniless orphan, Ryan at his death in 1928 left an estate valued at between $1 and 1/3 to 2 billion, more than that left by John Pierpont Morgan. Ryan's donations to Catholic causes, made mostly through his first wife, totalled more than $20 million.

The early hegira north also included various kinds of institutions to serve the elite world of Fifth Avenue. The fashionable St. Thomas Episcopal Church moved in 1870 to 53rd Street, its brown Gothic structure rebuilt in white limestone after a fire in 1905 destroyed the original building. Over its "bride's door" a carving of the dollar sign perpetuated an old tradition permitting carpenters or masons to leave some mark of social criticism in a remote stone or under a pew seat. The Fifth Avenue Bank on 44th Street offered a courtly atmosphere and comfortable furnishings to rich women who could maintain a minimum balance of $25,000 in their checking accounts.[6] Club life, an important element in the society of these years, was offered principally by the Union Club for merchants, bankers and politicians;

the Union League Club, a splinter group of pro-Lincoln sympathizers; and the Knickerbocker Club, sanctuary for descendants of early New York families. To an English visitor of the early 1880's, "the interior arrangements as to furniture and disposition of space of these clubs [were] far superior to anything in England." He also noted that "their adoption of the elevator enables them to have magnificent ...rooms high up... higher than our highest club houses," observing, however, "those I have seen are in some respects a trifle 'loud' according to English tastes."[7]

While the world of Fifth Avenue symbolized elegant New York, a sharp contrast was offered by the poverty of the residents of many of the streets to the east and west. Up to World War I, as large numbers of immigrants continued to flood New York City, slum districts inevitably spread northward to the Fifties and beyond, bringing far-reaching social and economic changes. In 1879, an attempt was made to improve the design of tenements built under an old law of 1867 which was rarely enforced. The new design left much to be desired, featuring as it did four apartments to a floor, with outside windows for only one room in each flat and a narrow airshaft between buildings. Nevertheless, great quantities of this design were executed and although a subsequent law of 1901 forbade construction of any more "Old Law" tenements, it did nothing to prevent their continued use. Meanwhile, with the growth of new industries (clothing, printing, food-processing, etc.) and the expansion of manufacturing enterprises, New York City by 1910 was producing over $1 and 1/3 billion worth of goods a year, one-tenth of the entire country's output.[8] Thus, if the newer immigrants who, after 1880, included numbers of unskilled Italians, suffered from poor pay and miserable working and living conditions, they were better off than the Irish and Germans of the 1840's for whom there had been no openings at all.[9]

Until 1898, when the first automobiles began to appear, Fifth Avenue dwellers continued to use the usual broughams and barouches and their, in many cases, Irish drivers, or the novel and expensive two-wheel hansom cabs available for hire.[10] A variety of other means of local transit were also available: the "El," electrified cable cars which had supplanted horsecars for surface travel, and, a year later, electric trolley cars when they were introduced. By October 24, 1904, New Yorkers could also take a five-cent subway ride, extending from City Hall up the east side to 42nd Street and Lexington Avenue, then across to Times Square and up Broadway to 145th Street. During its first 29 days of operation, this Interborough Rapid Transit Company, as it was named, carried 5,838,235 passengers who paid fares, in addition to smaller numbers who travelled on passes and the larger number of policemen and firemen who travelled free.[11]

Although the world of money, fashion and art of those housed in the great mansions on the Avenue was totally alien to that of the vast immigrant population whose world was shockingly revealed in Jacob Riis's *How the Other Half Lives*,[12] the new cathedral as parish church was called upon to meet the diverse needs of all its parishioners. In the long tradition of the Roman Catholic Church, the parish has been the place where the faithful encounter the priesthood, the teaching office and the sacramental system, as well as the other members of the Catholic community. The work of establishing such a parish at the cathedral was begun under the leadership of the first rector, Monsignor Quinn, with the help of his five assistants: Fathers James McQuirk, Cornelius Donovan, Charles E. McDonnell, Anthony Lammel and Michael J. Lavelle.[13]

For the estimated 12,000 parishioners, a variety of services were scheduled to meet their needs. The six Masses on Sunday were carried out with appropriate elegance, and emphasis was placed on the necessity of good preaching for the sermon that was part of each Mass. At the Solemn Mass on Sundays and other special occasions of the liturgical year, it was not unusual for a preacher of note in the city to be invited to give the sermon. Times for daily Mass were set and confessions were usually heard on Fridays and Saturdays and the eve of holydays, although special arrangements could be made at other times according to need. In the rectory, two priests were always on duty, one to look after visitors and the other to attend to sick calls.[14] Supervision of the cathedral school which opened in 1882 with Brother Isaac John Murphy, F.S.C., in charge of the boys' department, and Sister Mary Martha Hickey, S.C., of the girls, was another responsibility of the cathedral priests. Additional duties included the direction of catechism instruction and annual preparation of children for first confession, first communion and confirmation, as well as the direction of numerous societies for adults, such as the Holy Name, League of the Sacred Heart, and other parish devotional groups.[15] To these was added the management of the Cathedral Free Circulating Library which opened in 1888 and soon became more than a parish facility under the direction of Father Joseph Henry McMahon, who joined the cathedral staff in 1886.[16]

After the introduction of the Advent and Lenten Lecture Series they became an annual tradition, as did also May and October Devotions, the Solemn Mass on Thanksgiving and Memorial days, the New Year's Holy Name Society Mass and Communion Day, and the St. Patrick's Day Mass, followed by the traditional parade and review by civic, Church and other officials. Early arrangements had been made for the first public auction of the right of occupancy of pews in the cathedral, but confusion in interpreting the terms of these arrangements led the trustees to investigate the matter. The result was a statement clarifying the right of lessees to transmit to their heirs such rights, subject only to the payment of rent, such rent to be fixed by the Trustees from year to year, proportionate to the rent received from the other pews in the cathedral.[17]

Although the Third Synod of New York (1868) had forbidden the collection of money at the doors of the church on Sundays and holydays, door collections had become popular again by 1880 and the practice was adopted at the cathedral.[18] Over the years, a number of letters protesting this practice were received, including one in which the writer pointed out that Catholics, proud of their cathedral, were in the habit of inviting Protestant friends to attend services there. Not only was this done by those who held pews, but according to this letter, it was a common practice among Catholic business men who naturally expected that anyone they brought would be politely treated and given a seat. In this case the complainant was mollified by the reply he received stating that the charge for a campstool in the aisle for the occasion in question—High Mass on Easter Sunday—was not $2, as he had been told, but rather twenty-five to fifty cents.[19]

While the parish was taking shape under Monsignor Quinn, the cathedral itself was the setting for a series of events of the kind destined to be repeated again and again in future years, albeit involving different persons and different circumstances. On November 1, 1881, the first consecration of a bishop in the new cathedral took place with the elevation by Cardinal McCloskey of the Right Reverend Michael J. O'Farrell as Bishop of Trenton, New Jersey. On January 30, 1883, the mortal remains of Archbishop John Hughes were transferred from the vault in the old cathedral to be placed in the crypt beneath the high altar of the great cathedral he had founded twenty-five years before. That night the cathedral remained open to the public, while large numbers of people moved reverently past the bier on which the coffin reposed, many remaining for a time to keep watch and pray. The next morning, Cardinal McCloskey presided at the Pontifical Mass celebrated by Archbishop Corrigan who was attended by Monsignor Quinn and Vicar General Thomas Preston. Also present were the Bishops of Brooklyn, Albany and Rochester, as well as several members of the Rodrigue and Kelly families, relatives of Hughes.[20] Because the latter believed the occasion should be a cause for rejoicing "that the beautiful Cathedral which he saw only in a dim vision of the future. . . should so soon be ready to receive with honor and dignity his mortal remains," the cathedral was not draped in deep mourning.[21]

A joyous celebration in the cathedral the followng year on January 12, honored the cardinal's fiftieth anniversary of ordination. Present at the Solemn Pontifical Mass were Archbishop Corrigan and nine bishops, together with an immense gathering of both clergy and laity. It had been feared that the frail McCloskey would not live to observe this anniversary, for as one of the suffragan bishops put it "he has only been kept alive by great caution on his part, and great care on the part of his attendants." Appearing in the sanctuary in time to give the Pontifical Benediction, the cardinal listened to the several addresses made on behalf of the hierarchy, priests, religious and laity under his jurisdiction. After expressing his gratitude to those present, he contrasted the scene before him with the one that had occurred fifty years earlier in the old cathedral on the day of his ordination. Then, only one bishop and two priests occupied the sanctuary, and not many people were present in the pews.

Indeed, the growth was remarkable when one compares the statistics of 1834 with those of 1884. In the former year there were but six churches in the city, compared with sixty in 1884, while the number of priests in the diocese had increased from 20 in 1834 to 380 fifty years later. The

American hierarchy had also grown during the half-century from nine bishops and one archbishop in the United States to fifty-nine bishops, eleven archbishops and one cardinal-archbishop. McCloskey, responding to the fulsome praise of his administration, denied that the progress of the Church described in the several addresses was due to his efforts, attributing it rather to the "good will, zeal and generous cooperation of the clergy and laity of the diocese."[22]

In the months following this celebration, the health of the cardinal steadily declined, leading his coadjutor, Archbishop Corrigan, to send a message to Archbishop James Gibbons of Baltimore, asking him to arrange his schedule so that he might be free to preach at the funeral Mass. Gibbons' acceptance was sent three days before the cardinal's death on October 10, 1885.[23] While not unexpected, McCloskey's death brought a sense of great loss to the entire Church, as well as to countless New Yorkers and other Americans. Once again, Catholics and Protestants of the city flocked to the cathedral to pay their last respects, this time to the first American cardinal, whose body lay in state there for two days. An estimated 150,000 people passed before the bier, and the solemn funeral services on October 15 likewise brought an unprecedented number to the catheral. In his funeral oration, Archbishop Gibbons noted that grief at the loss of the Cardinal Archbishop of New York was not "confined to those who are of the household of the Faith. It extends to all classes and creeds of the community. The great heart of New York has mourned him . . . lamenting the death of one of its most illustrious and honored citizens." It was the preacher's opinion that neither wealth, nor power, nor rank, could command such heartfelt and universal respect" as that paid so spontaneously to New York's cardinal-archbishop.[24] After the final absolution, the coffin was placed in the vault next to that of his predecessor, under the high altar of the cathedral that stands as a monument to the combined vision and determination of the first two archbishops of New York. In keeping with the time-honored custom, McCloskey's red hat, or *galero*, was suspended from the sanctuary ceiling, high above his tomb.

Upon the death of McCloskey, Corrigan immediately became Archbishop of New York, having already had the advantage of five years' experience as coadjutor. During that time, he had been largely responsible for the success in 1883 of the Fourth Provincial Council of New York, and had gone to Rome to help prepare the agenda of the Third Plenary Council of Baltimore which he attended as representative of McCloskey when it opened in 1884.[25] All this work had been accomplished with little or no friction, but in less than a year after his succession to the see, serious conflicts began to develop and continued to plague his administration almost to the end. Among the most painful of these was Corrigan's uncompromising stand in regard to the views of one of his priests, Dr. Edward McGlynn, social reformer and pastor of the large and important St. Stephen's Church in the city. After repeated suspensions of McGlynn for his support of Henry George's single tax doctrine, Corrigan, early in 1887, removed the priest from his pastorate. When McGlynn, pleading poor health, refused to obey Leo XIII's summons to appear in Rome for a hearing of his case, he was excommunicated in July, 1887.

The storm raised by this and other issues of the time, such as the establishment of an apostolic delegation in the United States and that of state aid to parochial schools, was not confined to New York. Kept alive by debate within the Church and in the newspapers of the country at large, these issues were ultimately settled by the action of Rome. McGlynn was reinstated in December, 1892, after a hearing in Washington, D.C., before the papal ablegate, Archbishop Francesco Satolli, whose appointment as the first

Michael Augustine Corrigan
Archbishop of New York (1885-1902)

apostolic delegate to the United States was announced the following month.[26] Meanwhile, the thorny school controversy was aggravated when in April, 1892, the cardinals of the Propaganda in Rome judged that Archbishop John Ireland's Faribault-Stillwater plan could be tolerated. This plan of the Archbishop of St. Paul, Minnesota, embodied the principles of an arrangement which had been adopted in 1873 for the parish school of St. Peter's in Poughkeepsie, New York, whereby the parish school was rented for a nominal fee to the local school board. The latter provided for the teaching of secular subjects, while instruction in the Catholic religion was given after school hours.[27]

The success of this Poughkeepsie arrangement and its approval by Rome in 1874 led Father Quinn and representatives of more than fifty parish schools in the city to petition the board of education for its support in providing the 30,000 parochial school pupils with the benefits of the common school system. Although nothing came of this petition, the arrangement at the Poughkeepsie school continued to operate successfully until 1898, when it was ruled illegal by the state superintendent of public instruction, Charles R. Skinner.[28] Despite this precedent in his own archdiocese, Corrigan strongly opposed Ireland's plan for Faribault-Stillwater and interpreted Propaganda's decision as a condemnation of it. Debate on the school question heightened when, in November, 1892, Satolli as ablegate of the Holy See presented at the meeting in Corrigan's residence his fourteen propositions whereby the school controversy was to be settled in keeping with actual conditions. Accordingly, the parochial school should be established wherever possible; where this was not feasible, the bishop was encouraged to make arrangements similar to that of the Poughkeepsie plan; and where neither of the foregoing was practicable, provision was to be made for the religious instruction of Catholic children. Further debate on this issue ended when the Pope in his letter to Cardinal Gibbons of May 31, 1893, supported Satolli's propositions, at the same time making it clear that these in no way abrogated the parochial school legislation of the Third Plenary Council of Baltimore.[29]

Inevitably Corrigan's handling of the McGlynn case and his stand on the school question strained the archbishop's relations with McGlynn and his followers as well as with the supporters of Ireland. To one observer in New York, the situation appeared "outrageously polemical...where all calmness was lost and all the furies let loose."[30] Things worsened as the archbishop's own loyalty to Rome began to be questioned following sensational charges in the Chicago Sunday *Post* of January 8, 1893, that Corrigan and the priests at his cathedral residence had been supplying material and arguments for use in the attacks against Ireland and Satolli that had been appearing in newspapers across the country, particularly since McGlynn's restoration. Corrigan lost no time in writing to Cardinal Rampolla, Secretary of State, denying he had conspired in any way against the Holy See or been the inspiration for any of the letters or articles printed against the delegate or McGlynn. Nevertheless, the press was being supplied with material for the attacks against Ireland and Satolli by persons close to the archbishop. On February 11, 1893, Lavelle, who had become rector of the cathedral in 1887, admitted his part in the press campaign remarking that "if the other side was exploiting newspapers why should the archbishop be forbidden their use in airing his side of the issues."[31]

Peace was restored gradually with the passage of time. The issue of the Faribault-Stillwater experiment was closed when the school boards involved terminated the contracts by the fall of 1893.[32] When Corrigan took the initiative in August, 1893, and invited Satolli to officiate at St. Patrick's Cathedral for the feast of the Assumption, the occasion marked the beginning of regular visits of the delegate to the archiepiscopal residence on Madison Avenue.[33] After refusing McGlynn a parish in the city, Corrigan finally in January, 1895, appointed the priest to the pastorate of St. Mary's Church in Newburgh, New York.[34] Just five years later, the archbishop presided at Dr. McGlynn's obsequies which were held in the priest's old parish of St. Stephen's. That same year Corrigan visited Rome where he was well received by Leo XIII and Cardinal Rampolla, an indication that the events of the past decade had not permanently damaged his relations with the Holy See.[35] Some years later, Lavelle reminisced about these years in a letter to Denis O'Connell, who as rector of the North American College in Rome had acted as agent for Ireland and his supporters in the school controversy. Referring to their meeting in 1890 when "we were both young. . .and little dreamed of all the events that were to happen," Lavelle recalled his own "trials" and added "but they have done me good. . .and taught me some wisdom which I sorely lacked, with regard to character and the difficulty of knowing who is really good and who is the nave [sic.]."[36]

During these years of dissension over various key issues which put members of the American hierarchy in adversary positions on one or the other side of the current controversy, the cathedral parish and its rectory were experiencing developments of more local import. Monsignor Quinn, who had served the diocese so well under its first three archbishops, had been in poor health for some time. When it was learned that, on the advice of his doctor, Quinn was to spend some time in Europe, a group of the leading Catholics of the city arranged a testimonial dinner for him at Delmonico's. In appreciation of Quinn's labors that had made his "long sacerdotal career so honorable and meritorious," they presented him with "a small testimonial of their affection" and expressed their desire "that his journey be surrounded with all the comfort to which his years. . .and especially his great and successful priestly life entitled him."[37] Shortly after Quinn's arrival in Cork, Ireland, he informed Corrigan that his "cough was not worse" and he was "improved in other respects." Six months later, Quinn reported from Nice, France, that he thought his health had improved, but admitted "there is room for more."[38] Enroute home the following spring, Quinn died in Paris on April 15, 1887, and was subsequently buried in Calvary Cemetery, New York.[39]

Father Lavelle, who had been named temporary administrator in 1886 following Quinn's departure for Europe, became the second rector of the Cathedral in May, 1887.

Monsignor Michael Lavelle

Ordained at St. Joseph's Seminary in Troy, New York, just a month after the dedication of St. Patrick's, Lavelle's first assignment was to the cathedral where he was destined to spend all sixty years of his priestly life, fifty-two of them as its rector. A native New Yorker, Lavelle had studied at Manhattan College, receiving his Bachelor of Arts degree in 1873, and his Master of Arts two years later.[40] During his service at the cathedral, which spanned the successive administrations of five archbishops (four of whom became cardinals), countless improvements were made in the interior and exterior of the cathedral. The major ones, delineated in James Renwick's letter of April 16, 1888, recommended the restoration of elements of the original design including the Lady Chapel and sacristy, eliminated by Hughes to save costs, and the replacement of the plastered ceilings and wooden furring, substituted by McCloskey, with ones of galvanized iron on wrought iron frames.[41] Unfortunately, Renwick's death in June, 1895,[42] prevented him from seeing the implementation of his major recommendations since the financial resources of the cathedral did not permit plans for the Lady Chapel and sacristy to be drawn until 1899 and the work was not completed until 1906.

Over the years, the method of lighting the cathedral was improved a number of times, as was the system of heating and ventilation. A set of chimes cast by Paccard of Annecy, France, to be hung in the northern spire, was blessed by Corrigan on August 15, 1897. Each of the nineteen bells bears the name of a saint as well as that of the donor, the largest, named St. Patrick, being the gift of the cathedral parish.[43] By 1891, donors had made offers for all the altars for the side chapels, and Renwick was asked to supervise their construction so that a "certain amount of uniformity" would be insured.[44] Renwick himself designed one, that of St. John the Evangelist, which was given by Corrigan in memory of his predecessors in office, four of whom had been named John. The Stations of the Cross, carved in Holland in the Stoltzenberg ateliers, were of a cream-toned Caen stone, and three of them won prizes at the Chicago World's Fair of 1893 before the set was erected on the walls of the south and north transepts of the cathedral.[45] Of the many beautiful stained-glass windows, the earlier ones were executed in France and include two of St. Patrick, the titular one located over the south transept entrance telling the story of the saint's life in eighteen scenes. This was a gift of the Mott Street's "Old St. Patrick's Cathedral to the new."[46]

Various kinds of cathedral services were expanded during these years to accommodate the differing needs of a diverse congregation. One feature was the introduction of a 4:30 A.M. Mass on Christmas day to meet the needs of the many night workers in the city. In 1899 attendance at this service was reported to be greater than ever before, with the number of those receiving Holy Communion "very large."[47] This service was discontinued some years later, to be replaced by the Christmas Midnight Mass which was televised at the cathedral for the first time in 1948. For many years, this Mass was televised nationwide on Channel 4 (NBC); in 1980, a change to Channel 2 (CBS) reduced the viewing area to New York, Philadelphia, Chicago, Los Angeles and San Francisco. Organizations to aid the poor and the orphaned of the parish and the city multiplied and included the Cathedral Sewing Group, the Catholic Benevolent Legion, the Ladies of Charity and others. In 1902, the extraordinary works of charity of Miss Anne Leary, one of New York's so-called "Four Hundred," was recognized by Pope Leo XIII when he created her a countess, making Miss Leary the first American woman to bear a title bestowed by the Holy See.[48]

In the closing years of the 19th century, forms of popular

education such as that represented by the Chautauqua Literary and Scientific Circle, begun in 1878, multiplied. As an increasing number of Catholics became interested in adult education, Father McMahon opened the cathedral library to the general public in 1892, lengthening its hours of service to twelve a day, and gradually adding eleven branch libraries scattered throughout the city.[49] When, in 1896, a state charter was secured for the library,[50] it became entitled to public funding, making possible expanded services which continued until 1904 when it merged with other libraries to form the New York City Public Library.[51] Other educational programs sponsored by St. Patrick's included a school for catechists opened in 1900, and the Catholic Study Club for boys which numbered over 200 in 1903 and was called "one of the best and most fruitful works ever attempted in the cathedral."[52] The success of McMahon's Cathedral Library Reading Circle of New York led its founder, among others, to support a proposal for a meeting at the Catholic Club of New York in 1892, at which a working organization was set up for the Catholic Summer School of America, the first session of which was held a few months later in New London, Connecticut.[53]

The growing vitality of the parish was also demonstrated by the founding of such groups as the Cathedral Musical and Dramatic Society, the Drum and Fife Corps of the Cathedral, and the Cathedral Club which acquired its own clubhouse in 1893 and was a forerunner of larger groups such as the Catholic Club of New York, a Catholic version of the more fashionable Knickerbocker and Union League clubs. When the Guild of the Catholic Authors and Writers of America organized itself in 1898, the Cathedral Club was pleased to place its club rooms at the disposal of the Guild.[54] These years were also remarkable for the numbers of converts attracted to Catholicism, although they ceased to arouse as much public attention as did earlier ones that followed in the wake of the Oxford Movement and the conversion in 1845 of John Henry Newman. Conversions in New York in the latter part of the century included people from all walks of life, many of whom had become interested through the work of the Paulist Fathers whose founder, Isaac Hecker, was himself a convert in the 1840's. By 1903, the Paulists reported that "thousands are joining the Catholic Church...the rate of conversion in the Archdiocese of New York is 5,000 a year." The New York Apostolic Band of Diocesan Priests, in addition to preaching and hearing confessions, also gave missions to non-Catholics, as a result of which 319 were received into the Church during 1905.[55]

From the outset, music was an important part of the services at the cathedral and attracted non-Catholics as well as the parishioners and other Catholics of the city. In the early years it was provided by quartet choirs and orchestral ensembles, in keeping with the operatic style then in vogue, In 1904, however, in accordance with the wishes of Pope Pius X, instructions were issued to all churches in the archdiocese that Gregorian music was "to be restored...to its high place of honor," and that "the proper of the Mass and the antiphons, etc. of Vespers be rendered according to the same." As might be expected, the change did not recommend itself to some parishioners for whom the lack of singers trained in Gregorian chant only added to their discomfort. A measure of relief was afforded when a choir composed of the clergy was formed to study Plain Song and to provide the singing on the occasions of priests' requiems and other important ceremonies at the cathedral.[56]

The task of making the cathedral parish self-supporting during these years proved to be an impossible one. From the beginning, yearly income from the parish proved inadequate to take care of the increasing operating expenses so that by 1894 each year showed a deficit varying from

$10,000 to more than $20,000. This did not include annual interest payments which, if added, would increase the deficit by some $16,000 yearly, not to mention payments on account of principal of mortgage, all of which had to be paid by the cathedral trustees constituting "a serious drain on their treasury." In presenting this to Lavelle, the trustees urged him to place the problem clearly before the parishioners, feeling sure that the latter "will be both able and willing to contribute whatever may be necessary to make the Cathedral self-supporting."[57] Lavelle acted immediately and *The Catholic News* of November 4, 1894, carried the rector's letter outlining the pressing need to make the cathedral self-supporting. Reminding his readers that "the cost of maintaining a church like this is always very great especially when conducted in a liberal fashion which is characteristic of the cathedral with a large and completely organized school, a superior choir and various charitable and benevolent works," he also called their attention to the annual interest payment of $16,000 and an indebtedness of $400,000. A bazaar, held the following month at the Grand Central Palace of Industry at 44th Street and Lexington Avenue, which lasted for two weeks, made it possible for the rector to report back to the trustees that he had "placed $25,000 to the credit of the Board." A year later, Lavelle forwarded to the trustees a check for $12,000, the proceeds from a special collection taken up in the cathedral on Sunday, December 1, 1895, to which sum the trustees added $13,000, the total to be "paid on account of the Cathedral mortgage on or before May 15, 1896."[58] However, despite continuing effort to insure that cathedral expenses were matched by parish income, the battle was never completely won.

Finances were not Lavelle's only problem during the closing years of the century when friction developed between two members of his own household which he was unable to resolve. In writing of this problem to Corrigan, the rector suggested that the archbishop interview the two priests involved, Fathers William J. B. Daly and Joseph H. McMahon, adding that the two priests were said to have been "great friends in the seminary" and that he believed them to be "able, presentable and pious men." Indeed both had "exposed their lives," Daly as chaplain of the 69th Regiment by going with the American troops during the brief Spanish-American War of 1898 "to hardship and possible death," and McMahon by "volunteering to go to Camp Wickoff last September." Denying that he had shown partiality towards any of his priests, Lavelle declared his one ambition was to be the archbishop's "executive officer" in making St. Patrick's "the greatest Church in the world, not in pomp and show... but in practical utility and in solid results." Declaring that "the priest who desires to help most ... to this end can have my whole heart," but "he who tries to aid less, can have it in a minor degree [and] should anyone be wrapped in selfishness so as to assist not at all, that man... could have no part whatsoever in my real life." To end the contention, Lavelle suggested that the archbishop appoint Daly first assistant to the rector with responsibility for a specified number of duties, thereby lightening Lavelle's burden. As for McMahon, Lavelle suggested that Corrigan have a "friendly chat," assuring the priest of the appreciation of the archbishop and the rector, but also, "quoting Shakespeare" remind the priest that "It is great to have the strength of a lion, but not to use it like a lion."[59]

Apparently the friction in the rectory continued, for two years later McMahon wrote to Corrigan that although he disliked to "intrude my personal affairs when I know you have so much to bother you," he was "afraid that there will be another row this week between the Rector and myself, and I should like to ask if there is any way by which I could be spared the unnecessary humiliation to which I am subjected." McMahon listed a number of grievances among which was the failure of the rector to honor McMahon's request that an announcement be made of the usual novena in preparation for the feast of the Sacred Heart, although the cathedral "pulpit is laden with announcements of social entertainments." Morever, he informed Corrigan that he had not received "one dollar of salary since October, making $300 due me, plus $500 for stationery for the Cathedral Library Association, "held up I suppose in order to cripple me," as well as "requiem perquisites for two years prior to 1896." Assuring the archbishop that he "had not been wanting in patience," he acknowledged that he was getting discouraged because "in order to keep out of mischief, I have to live almost the life of a recluse in the Rectory, keeping out of it all I can to preserve my peace of mind."[60]

In 1901, McMahon became the founder and pastor of a parish to be established uptown under the patronage of Our Lady of Lourdes, a project he successfully launched on a site between Convent and Amsterdam Avenues and 142nd and 143rd Streets while continuing his association with the Cathedral Library. When friction again developed between Lavelle and himself, he moved the office and main library from 50th Street to 86th Street and Amsterdam Avenue "to spare Father Lavelle the anxiety expressed that my presence on 50th Street would corrupt his school children." Lavelle then tried to set up a library at 50th Street as an independent concern without regard to the system McMahon had built up, causing the latter to point out the legal complications arising from this action, not to mention "the disgrace and scandal given to the library authorities to see us quarreling amongst ourselves when we should be a unit. . . resisting the encroachment of our enemies."[61] This issue was laid to rest with the merger of the Cathedral Library in 1904 to form the New York City Public Library. Despite these differences, McMahon and Lavelle were both among the founders of the

Catholic Summer School of America, as well as supporters
of The Catholic University of America. Both were honored
by the Church, McMahon being named a domestic prelate
in 1921, while Lavelle, who had received similar recognition
in 1904, was made a prothonotary apostolic in 1929.[62]

Meanwhile, Corrigan, who had initiated plans for the
construction of the Lady Chapel, was looking forward to its
completion so that a date might be set for the consecration
of the cathedral. In 1900, he wrote to the trustees advising
them that he would like the consecration to take place in
May, 1904, the 25th anniversary of the opening of the
cathedral.[63] Two years later, however, the archbishop,
whose health had never been robust, failed to recover from a
fall he suffered in late February while going from his residence to the cathedral to make his usual evening visit. In the

Easter Sunday 1904

dim light he failed to see the excavation made in preparation for the construction of the Lady Chapel and sacristy below, and only saved himself from falling the twenty-five feet to the cellar by catching on to a beam supporting the flooring. His cries brought several attendants to his assistance and following treatment for shock and bruises, he was expected to recover fully even after subsequently developing pneumonia. His sudden death from a heart attack shortly after 11:00 P.M. on May 5, 1902, came as a great shock to all.[64]

Cardinal Gibbons celebrated the funeral Mass in St. Patrick's at which Archbishop Ryan preached, likening his deceased friend to "a rock gently yielding, mossy on the surface," underneath which "strength and power and immovability of principle were found."[65] Following the absolutions, the coffin bearing the remains of New York's third archbishop was carried to the vault under the high altar to join those of his predecessors. The police estimated that seven to eight thousand persons were in the cathedral for the services, while some fifteen thousand had stood in the streets around the cathedral to watch the procession from the Boland Trade School (later used for Cathedral College) to the cathedral. The press of the day reported many details of the archbishop's career, mentioning the many churches built during his administration, the growth of the clergy, the expansion of the parochial school system, and his "crowning work," the establishment of St. Joseph's Seminary at Dunwoodie at a cost (with the land) of nearly a million dollars. Corrigan himself had contributed $100,000 from his private fortune to this cause and just four years before his death, on the occasion of the twenty-fifth anniversary of his consecration, the outstanding mortgage of $250,000 on the seminary was paid off by contributions from the clergy and people of the diocese as a testimonial to their archbishop.[66]

Among Corrigan's personal friends whose reactions to

the news of his death were reported in the press, W. Bourke Cochran was quoted as saying his personal grief was "deepened by the fact that I will never have the chance to repeat to him my conversation with the Holy Father in Rome three weeks ago in which...I remember his saying "he is a great prelate, a holy man." John D. Crimmins, a trustee of the cathedral, described Corrigan as "a beautiful character ...rigid in the performance of requirements, but when it was in place to throw off the serious side, then...you saw the lovely, genteel and happy man...."[67] However, one *In Memoriam*, signed "The Secretary," described the deceased as "honest...well meaning" but added "there were kinks" in his character...Living in the twentieth century he had traits, theories and prejudices best suited to the thirteenth."[68] Some four months after Corrigan's death, John M. Farley, who had served as auxiliary bishop since 1895, as well as pastor of St. Gabriel's Church in New York from 1891, was named Archbishop of New York on September 15, 1902. Following the arrival of the pallium from Rome, it was conferred upon Farley by the Apostolic Delegate, the Most Reverend Diomede Falconio, in a solemn ceremony on August 12, 1903.[69]

CHAPTER IV
St. Patrick's Educational Programs

The early decades of the cathedral's history witnessed the introduction of a variety of educational programs to serve the Catholics of the parish and of the city. The first rector, Monsignor Quinn, initiated plans for the construction of a red brick school building on lots purchased at 111 and 113 East 50th Street, between Lexington and Park Avenues. Completed in 1882 at a cost of $90,000,[1] the building was ready for occupancy that September and opened with a registration of 570 boys and 555 girls.[2] The previous March, a house at 248 East 49th Street had been purchased to be used as a residence for the Brothers of the Christian Schools who would staff the boys' department of cathedral school. After a thorough renovation, the house was ready to receive the Brothers in early September, 1882, and it continued to be their home during the fifty-nine years of their service at the cathedral school. Although their arrival in what at the time was a "comparatively Jewish district" was not hailed with any great enthusiasm by the more orthodox families of the area, the brothers from the beginning met with only kindness from one neighboring Jewish family. On the first day of the brothers' occupancy of No. 248, when lunch was ready to be served and it was discovered that there were no knives or forks to be found in the house, an appeal was made to the Jewish family at No. 246 who willingly loaned them the necessary cutlery.[3]

Brother Isaac John Murphy, F.S.C., a long-time friend of Quinn, was appointed the first director of the boys' department of the cathedral school, where his first teaching staff included Brothers Alician Joseph Daly, Binen Alphonsus Barrete, Euthemius Alban English and Albinus Peter Walsh for the upper classes. Secular teachers were engaged to teach the younger boys. Over the years, Brother Isaac John's successors as director of the boys' department of the school included Brothers Benignus Austin McGeehan (1889-98), Blaise Austin Roach (1898-1902; 1915-16),[4] Arnold Edward Saunders (1902-04), Alban Faber Shallew (1904-12), Adelbert Patrick Neville (1912-15; 1919-22), Binen Michael Lenihan (1916-19), Cornelius Luke Pryor (1922-27), and Amandus Henry Kargl (1927-29). Until 1904, the cathedral school offered only a grammar school program, but that year brought the introduction of commercial studies which subsequently developed into a two-year high school course. By the 1920's, however, the complexity of life in the metropolis demanded that a longer period of study be provided not only for the select few, but for all the youth of the city. Thus in 1925, the cathedral school adopted a full four-year academic program which included courses in Latin and biology.[5]

With the demolition of the original school building in July, 1926 to make room for a new diocesan girls' high school, the boys' high school program was moved to a new location at 189 East 76th Street. There, under the successive administrations of Brothers Albert George Sweeney, Andrew Philip Girard, Bernard of Mary Ryan and Adelphus Joseph Veno, the school achieved an enviable reputation for the number of scholarships won annually by its students. In 1941 when Cardinal Spellman launched a central diocesan high school system, the 76th Street boys' annex of Cathedral High School was merged with the new Cardinal Hayes Memorial High School and, after nearly six decades of service, the Christian Brothers withdrew from the cathedral parish.[6] The house on East 49th Street where the brothers had lived for so many years was sold in 1942 for $9,000.[7] Meanwhile, the boys' grammar school had been housed, together with that of the girls', at 117 East 50th Street, where the former was staffed by the brothers and lay teachers until 1929. Thereafter, the dwindling enrollment in both departments of the parochial school (205 boys and 190 girls by 1931) resulted in all classes being taken over by lay teachers and the Sisters of Charity, whose members had taught in the girls' department since 1882.[8]

From its inception, cathedral boys' school enjoyed an excellent reputation, ranking first among the parochial schools of the city in drawing. At the World's Industrial and Cotton Centennial Exposition held in New Orleans in 1884, among the thirty-seven parochial schools represented, the cathedral school's exhibit received special mention as "the neatest and most excellent work. Its illustrated and descriptive albums of the Holy Land, the Jeannette Expedition and the Geological Formation of New York State, and one of composition are greatly admired." More than a thousand of the boys' drawings were exhibited at the Columbian Exposition held in Chicago in 1893, the same year the school won two appointments to West Point in a competition held for twenty-five students from the schools of the 13th and 14th Congressional Districts of the city. Eight boys from the cathedral school entered the contest, together with representatives from City College and the public and private schools of the two districts. When the results were available, cathedral boys had captured first, second and third places, with the other five cathedral entrants not too far behind. Although first place had been won by Joseph L. Hunt, who had achieved a grade of 93, a physical disability prevented him from receiving one of the two cadetships which, accordingly, were awarded to his classmates, John H. Hughes and

Timothy M. Coughlin, whose grades in the competition were 92 and 91, respectively.[9]

These and other awards won by the children of the cathedral school meant a great deal to them and to their families who "never displayed any evidence of being much blessed with this world's goods." Indeed, poverty was an all too familiar condition of life to the Catholics of the city whose children consequently knew neither the "advantages nor disadvantages attached to a life of ease." Nevertheless, the children attending the cathedral school had, for the most part, been spared poverty "of the meaner sort," so that their lives were characterized by a degree of "independence and dignity." Thus the boys exhibited an amazing ability to emerge successfully from their struggle with unfavorable surroundings. Their spirit of achievement was not limited to the academic field, but also found its way into athletics, and after graduation relatively few failed to achieve "a cheerful prosperity and an enviable eminence among their fellows," as well as an "edifying attachment to things Catholic and a striking loyalty to their teachers." The school's alumni include some twenty-five priests and at least ten Christian Brothers.[10]

From the earliest years, a number of school-related organizations and activities supplemented the formal academic program, while serving also to foster close faculty relations with Cathedral's students, parents and alumni. The practice of opening the school year with the Mass of the Holy Spirit brought teachers and students together in the beautiful cathedral that was within walking distance of the school building. The cathedral was also the setting for such school events as the annual Lenten mission and the Benediction service of the Archconfraternity of the Infant Jesus held each May.[11] In 1888, the Cathedral Club had been founded by Brother Isaac John, while a later director of the school, Brother Blaise Austin, organized the Cathedral School

Alumni Association, which held the first of its annual communion breakfasts in 1901. In 1939, these two associations jointly sponsored a Communion breakfast at the Hotel Pierre to celebrate the 50th anniversary of the founding of Cathedral Club. The Parents' Association, launched in 1932 by Brother Andrew Philip as director of the 76th Street high school annex, sponsored socials and other fund-raising activities, including a Spring dance and an annual card party, the proceeds of which were given to the brothers and generally used to keep the 48th Street residence in good repair.[12]

Through the early decades of the twentieth century, the cathedral school continued to win recognition for the academic success of its students. In a public contest sponsored by the Knights of Columbus in 1919, the boys' department won every medal offered for the best essays. Three years later, a boy from Cathedral received the coveted honor of first place in the mental arithmetic examination open to all 7th grade pupils in the city, while a fellow student in the 8th grade achieved fourth place in a competitive examination in spelling for 8th graders in the city. Achievements of this kind tended to attract good students to the school with the result that by the opening of the school year in 1923, the enrollment was greater than in any preceding year, and students who tried to register during the first week of classes had to be turned away for lack of space.[13]

When the boys' high school was moved in 1926 to the 76th Street building, every effort was made to preserve the high standards of the old school, despite the inadequacies of the physical plant at the new site. When, in the early 1930's, Brother Andrew Philip introduced a competitive entrance examination, the scholastic standing of the high school improved considerably. By 1936, instead of two freshman classes entering each year, only one class of about 45 was admitted, since the former practice of students dropping out after the second year had entirely ceased and available space permitted of only one freshman, two sophomore, two junior and one senior class for a student body of about 250. The course of study included Religion (4 years), English (4 years), Latin (3 years), Ancient and American History, Civics and Economic Citizenship, Biology and Physics, Elementary and Intermediate Algebra, Plane and Solid Geometry and Trigonometry.

The 1939 graduating class of seventy-five was the largest in the history of the school and all received College Entrance Diplomas, most with honor (90% or higher) and the remainder with credit (85%-90%), with eight winning New York State Regents' Scholarships. By comparison, the 1940 and 1941 graduating classes were small, numbering only thirty-six in each year. Rumors that the school was to be closed had been circulating for some months, causing unrest among the students, their parents, the alumni and the brothers. By April, 1941, it was officially confirmed that the school would close that June and students who wished might continue their studies at the new Cardinal Hayes Memorial High School. As a consequence, the joy of the final commencement exercises was somewhat muted by a note of sadness, even though the graduates themselves were not directly affected by the situation. In July, all the records of the school were transferred to St. Bernard's School to be turned over in September to Cardinal Hayes High School.[14]

In the girls' department of the cathedral school, registration had reached 675 by 1885, the year Sister Mary Martha Hickey, the first director, was replaced by Sister Mary Raymond Hennessey, who had taught in the school since its opening.[15] Twenty years later, with the support of the cathedral's rector, Monsignor Lavelle, Sister Mary Raymond played an important part in the establishment of Cathedral Girls' High School, of which she remained in charge until 1919.[16] For many years, Sister Mary Raymond had prepared students at cathedral school for the entrance examinations to Normal College, later Hunter College; thus the twenty-eight graduates of 1897, all under fifteen years of age, planned to enter Normal College or high school.[17] Countrywide, between 1890 and 1920, the percentage of American youth enrolling in high school had risen from six percent to thirty percent, reaching more than sixty-five percent by 1940.[18] However, with the increase in the number of high schools, entrance requirements for Normal College became much more exacting, and in 1901 College Board examinations were introduced, establishing uniform standards for all secondary schools and specifying the subjects and number of units required for college entrance.

Accordingly, in 1905, Monsignor Lavelle launched a tuition-free parochial high school in the same building that housed the grammar school, a modest beginning for what was to become by 1925 the first archdiocesan high school in New York. At its inception, however, so few cathedral parishioners realized the need of a high school education for girls, that only a canvass of the parish by Sisters Mary Raymond and Regina Rose Brull in the spring of 1905, urging parents to register their daughters for the freshman class, succeeded in attracting thirty-two students to the first class that opened in September. The high school faculty for the first year consisted of Sisters Mary Raymond, Regina Rose and Marie Annette Scanlon; as an additional class was added each September, Sisters Rose Mercedes Gillespie, Mary Alacoque Velton, Miriam Josita McKenna and Mary Giovanni Murphy joined the high school staff of cathedral.[19] By the fourth year enrollment had reached 154, including 20 in the 4th year, 12 in the 3rd, 32 in 2nd, and 90 in the first year.[20]

In 1907, the Regents of the University of the State of New York granted cathedral a provisional charter for a three-year high school, followed in 1908 by one for a four-year school. In 1910, the high school department received its final and permanent charter and changed the name from

St. Patrick's is above all a place of worship

Cathedral School to Cathedral High School.[21] The first commencement, held in the school auditorium in 1909, was presided over by Lavelle who in his capacity as rector had through the years made weekly visits to his cathedral school. Of the seventeen graduates of 1909, four went on to normal school and six to college. By 1914, in a graduating class of twenty members, thirteen earned New York State Scholarships at a time when such awards were not numerous.[22] Although pupils from other parishes began to be admitted, Cathedral High School remained for some twenty years a parochial institution, with the parish bearing the expenses of its operation, assisted only by the voluntary donations of some of its students.[23] During these years, the school's reputation for high scholarship became firmly established and would be faithfully carried on when, after 1927, it became an archdiocesan facility.

Sister Marie Victoire Kerby, who succeeded Sister Mary Raymond in 1919, would preside over what became a transition period for the school. In the era of prosperity between the end of World War I and the depression of 1929, diocesan high schools generally emerged as the most efficient and least expensive method of meeting the increasing demand for high school facilities. In New York, the decision was finally made to build such a school on the site already occupied by the cathedral school. After the demolition in 1926 of one section of the old building, construction began on the new archdiocesan school to be known as Cathedral High School, Archbishop Hughes Memorial. When completed, the building occupied the entire northwest corner of Lexington Avenue and 50th Street and extended practically a quarter of the block toward Park Avenue. Swept away in the course of this project, in addition to the original school building, were six apartment houses on Lexington Avenue and the Cathedral Branch of the New York Public Library, a landmark for many years.[24]

In September, 1927, Cathedral High School's staff of

nineteen sisters and three lay teachers, together with a student body of 800, moved from the south side of the old building to the completed north half of the new high school. The elementary grades also moved there, occupying space on the first floor, so that the southern portion of the old building could be razed to permit completion of the remainder of the new structure. By the end of the ensuing year, the new building was entirely completed and graduation was held there even though the eight-story structure had not yet been dedicated. That ceremony was performed the following October 10th by Cardinal Hayes and, for many years thereafter, Cathedral High School remained the only diocesan high school in New York, its Gothic tower rising far above the three- and four-story buildings of the neighborhood, many of which housed shopkeepers who lived above their stores.[25] As a diocesan facility, Cathedral High School continued to expand over the years, necessitating the opening of branch schools to accommodate an ever-increasing registration, while still maintaining a consistently high standard of scholarship.

Meanwhile, however, the cathedral grammar school faced an uncertain future as the flight of residents from the midtown area continued to grow. The school, dependent for pupils on the children from homes on the local streets, experienced a steady decline in enrollment. By 1930, the Christian Brothers had withdrawn from the teaching staff of the grammar school, where the faculty for both the boys' and girls' classes consisted of the Sisters of Charity and lay teachers. As registration continued to drop, reaching only 395 by 1931, and less than 300 in 1939, its closing was inevitable; thus by 1942 this parish facility which had served countless children since 1882 ceased to exist. Through the ensuing decades, however, the parish provided "Sunday School" classes, held in Cathedral High School and taught by the Sisters of Charity, "for all children not attending Catholic grammar or high school."[26]

During the years that the cathedral schools were expanding their programs for the Catholic youth of the city, efforts were also being made to extend educational opportunities for adults. Among those of the late nineteenth century was a program known as "The Cathedral Library University Extension Lectures" which, under Father McMahon, had grown out of his Cathedral Library Reading Circle of New York. Offered for the first time in 1897, the lectures proved so successful that McMahon's schedule for the following year included three courses on psychology to be taught by himself and two professors from The Catholic University of America: Drs. Edward A. Pace and Edmund T. Shanahan.[27] These lectures, intended primarily to prepare teachers to meet New York State certification requirements, filled a real need in the city. Conditions at the time were such that only those possessing a college degree, or who had completed sixty hours of work in an approved college or university, were eligible for certain state licenses. While Catholic men could meet this requirement by attending the College of St. Francis Xavier in New York, only non-Catholic institutions were available in the city to Catholic women who desired similar training and certification.

In 1902, at the suggestion of McMahon,[28] a committee of the trustees of The Catholic University of America, took the first steps towards the establishment of an Institute of Pedagogy in New York City open to women. When members of the University Senate expressed opposition to the project on the ground that the University itself lacked a department of pedagogy, they were overruled at the April, 1902, meeting of the University's Board of Trustees. Due in large part to the strong support of one of the trustees, Bishop John Lancaster Spalding of Peoria, Illinois, McMahon's proposal was "endorsed heartily and considered a very efficient way to bring the work of The Catholic University and of its financial needs to the notice of the public."[29]

McMahon, delighted when news of the trustees' action reached him, reported that the Jesuits had offered St. Francis Xavier College in the city for the use of the Institute program, adding "so that heavy item of expense is removed."[30] By October, 118 teachers had registered for the Institute, to which the University Rector, Thomas J. Conaty, had appointed Pace as the first dean.[31]

During the ensuing years, as the registration continued to grow, Pace and the Washington members of his Institute faculty traveled to New York each week to conduct their classes.[32] Meanwhile, McMahon had gathered the names of qualified local men willing to take over additional courses as needed.[33] By 1907, largely through the efforts of Pace and Thomas E. Shields, the University trustees had approved a proposal for the establishment there of a Department of Education. As a consequence, the New York Institute, expanded in 1907 to include graduate extension courses, attracted the largest attendance of any department of education in the New York area. As Pace and Shields developed the program of standardization and curriculum affiliation, institutes of like nature in other cities of the country were encouraged to make arrangements for a similar association with the University.[34]

Still another outgrowth of the reading circle movement was the Catholic Summer School of America, the first sponsors of which had included both Lavelle and McMahon of the cathedral staff. When a permanent site for the school was found at Cliff Haven, New York, the administration building was built in 1894, at a cost of about $25,000.[35] Among the officers of the Summer School for 1894 were Joseph H. McMahon, Vice-President, and Thomas J. Conaty, President, who was described by a Summer School lecturer as a "sort of Archbishop Ireland, with New England checks and balances so to speak."[36] Following his appointment by Pope Leo XIII to the rectorship of The Catholic University of America, Conaty, in January, 1897, resigned from his Summer School responsibilities. The latter were assumed by Lavelle who continued to serve as president until the end of the 1903 session. During this seven-year administration of Lavelle, the Summer School continued to prosper, increasing to some 2,480 participants in 1898 and 5,281 in 1903. By the end of the first decade of the twentieth century, this center of Catholic popular education was firmly established. According to one public school man, it "along with the founding of the Catholic University and the beginning of the publication of the Catholic Encyclopedia" constituted "the three greatest events in American Catholic history during the twenty-five years just past, considered from the intellectual standpoint."[37]

Any consideration of the intellectual climate of these years, however, should not overlook the launching of the scholarly but short-lived *New York Review* which, sponsored by Archbishop Farley, appeared for the first time in the summer of 1905.[38] Under the editorship of the Reverend James F. Driscoll, S.S., Rector of St. Joseph's Seminary, Dunwoodie, and two priest members of the seminary faculty, the publication was designed "to discuss in a scholarly way...the various questions with which the modern Christian apologist has to deal—mainly those pertaining to Scripture and Philosophy." In presenting reviews of material bearing on theology, scripture, philosophy and related sciences, the editors hoped to "draw attention to the needs of the present intellectual situation in matters of religious belief." Driscoll's revision of the program of studies at Dunwoodie was likewise boldly designed "to produce priests who were not only pious, but cultivated in the things of the mind...and aware of what was happening on the American and world scenes, intellectually, culturally and socially." To this end he invited to Dunwoodie Protestant as well as Catholic guest lecturers who could speak with authority on such pertinent topics as "The Catholic Church and Twentieth Century Thought," "Socialism," etc.[39]

For a brief time, these attempts to support the kind of in-depth study of theology and scripture associated with the best of European scholarship placed New York in the forefront of a budding intellectual movement in the American Church. But the issue of modernism,[40] condemned by Pope Pius X in his 1907 encyclical *Pascendi Dominici gregis*, soon stifled scholarly efforts of this kind. Early in 1908, the apostolic delegate, Archbishop Diomede Falconio, wrote to Farley declaring that the most recent issue of the *Review* contained material in violation of the encyclical *Pascendi*. Although Farley initially defended the *Review* against the delegate's charges, the publication ceased with the May-June, 1908, issue in which the editors announced its discontinuance, citing lack of financial support as the reason.[41] Not until 1940 with the appearance of *Theological Studies*, the Jesuit-edited quarterly, did the Catholic community of the United States again have a publication equal to that of the *New York Review*.

The early years of the twentieth century also saw the opening of a preparatory seminary which would, so Archbishop Farley stated, "in conjunction with our grand theological seminary at Dunwoodie...render complete and perfect the system of ecclesiastical education in the diocese." Its location in the very shadow of the cathedral reflected the then widely held belief that "the perfect candidate for Holy Orders is the youth whom the Bishop has known and watched over from the tender years of his boyhood."[42] Thus in September, 1903, Cathedral College opened in the renovated building of the Boland Trade School on the old site of the Roman Catholic Orphan Asylum on Madison Avenue, between 51st and 52nd Streets.[43] The previous month, the chancery offices of the archdiocese had moved from the old headquarters on Mulberry Street to the first floor of this building in which Cathedral College would be located for nearly forty years. Farley appointed his chancellor, the Reverend Patrick J. Hayes, first president of the college, where two of the cathedral priests, Fathers Thomas F. Murphy and Richard O. Hughes, served as the faculty for the first class of about fifty students who had passed the entrance examinations. Additional faculty, including laymen, were to be added as required.[44]

Other educational projects, support for which was provided by those connected with the cathedral of New York, included—in addition to such local institutions as a school for the blind and an institute for the training of women in skills necessary for home economics, dressmaking, secretarial work and fashion merchandising—The Catholic University of America in Washington, D.C. During Corrigan's episcopate in New York, Farley had acted as the first secretary of the hierarchy's committee for the founding of the Washington University;[45] following his appointment as Corrigan's successor, the new archbishop lost no time in personally taking up the cause of the University, also making it clear to his clergy that he expected their enthusiastic support to match his own.[46]

For one of Farley's priests, Joseph H. McMahon of the Cathedral Library, no prodding was necessary for, at the request of Cardinal Gibbons, he had already undertaken a tour of the country in what proved a rather unsuccessful attempt to raise funds for the University's operating expenses.[47] However, with the inauguration of a new national archdiocesan collection for the University, the yearly returns from New York (1903-1908) were among the largest in the country. Farley was elected to serve on the University's Board of Trustees following Monsignor Denis J. O'Connell's appointment in 1903 as third rector of that institution. When, in 1907, it was decided to enlarge the board by bringing in additional members who would be devoted to its cause, Monsignor Lavelle was among those invited.[48]

Through the efforts of a blind teacher, Miss Margaret Coffey, helped by Joseph M. Stadelman, a Jesuit of St.

Francis Xavier College in the city, the first school for the blind opened in 1904 in a five-room apartment on West 21st Street. When this work was brought to the attention of Farley, he referred the matter to Lavelle who was then vicar general as well as rector of the cathedral. In 1908, with the latter's help, the school with its twelve children moved to 223 West 15th Street and was incorporated the following year as the Catholic Institute for the Blind. When the Dominican Sisters of Blauvelt took over the direction of the school, Miss Coffey remained as teacher and adviser until poor health caused her to retire to her home in Massachusetts where she died in January, 1942. Meanwhile, in 1916, the school moved into the existing buildings of the former Stickney estate at 221st Street and Paulding Avenue in the Bronx, where in 1930 modern fireproof buildings were constructed to house the boys and girls, and soon after a new administration building was added. In July, 1938, the name of the institution was changed to The Lavelle School for the Blind, in honor of the cathedral's rector, whose death the following year was keenly felt by all associated with the school.[49]

Grace Institute, founded in 1897 by a New York Catholic businessman and cathedral trustee, William R. Grace, was the city's first free vocational school for young women. The Irish-born Grace had made a fortune in Peru before arriving in New York where he organized the shipping firm of W. R. Grace and Company while continuing to acquire valuable silver mines, oil and mineral land, railroad properties, etc. By 1880, when he became the first Catholic to be elected Mayor of New York, Grace was a very wealthy man and his reform administration of the city was judged to have "brought credit to the Irish-Americans."[50] After Grace purchased a house on West 60th Street for the Institute and secured the Sisters of Charity to staff it, the first Mass in the chapel there on February 2, 1897, was attended by several members of the Grace family as well as the sisters. Among the latter were Sister Marie Dolores Van Rensselaer, first superior of the Institute community, which included Sisters Marie Victor Francis who taught sewing, Rose Michael O'Shea dressmaking, and Agnes Mary Cahill cooking.[51] Daytime classes were scheduled for housewives, while evening classes were made available for working girls.

When, later, a secretarial department was added, its excellent reputation was further enhanced when the Institute students won the Pitman Cup for shorthand in twenty-five successive years. By 1960, approximately 70,000 girls and women had completed courses in Grace Institute, while the registration for the 1959-60 year totaled 1,374, of whom 676 received certificates of graduation or diplomas in June. By this time, however, the neighborhood had witnessed considerable demolition, as plans for the Lincoln Square Development were implemented. Thus, the school, with the support of Mr. Peter Grace, then President of W. R. Grace and Company, moved to a new twelve-story structure between 64th and 65th Streets, Second and Third Avenues, where the Institute would occupy the first three floors, with a separate entrance at 1233 Second Avenue for their use.[52] This building was dedicated and blessed by Cardinal Spellman in September, 1963.[53]

The decades between 1890 and 1930, during which almost sixteen million immigrants entered the United States via the port of New York, brought many changes to the city. By 1892, the inadequacy of the two existing immigration stations—one at Castle Garden near the Battery and the other on Ward's Island in the East River—led to the transfer of immigration control from the State to the Federal Government. Ellis Island in Upper New York Bay was then chosen as the new immigration station and it served until 1954 as the main gateway to America for all steerage-class immigrants, who numbered over twelve million between 1892-1925. These unfortunates were taken off their ships before they reached dock and transferred by barge to Ellis

Island, "the Island of Tears," where they were herded from place to place, tested for contagious diseases and endlessly questioned about such personal matters as their morality, etc. In 1907 alone, more than a million immigrants endured this processing, many of whom came from southern and eastern Europe, the so-called "new immigrants," and were practically penniless after spending their life-savings for a one-way ticket. Among those who passed the inspection, some suffered the further indignity of having the officials arbitrarily assign them new names, either by anglicizing their real ones or by giving them new ones which reflected their place of origin. Far worse, however, was the fate of those who were denied admission, for the resulting anguish led some to commit suicide rather than be sent back to their native country.[54]

The creation of Greater New York on January 1, 1898, was the result of discussions and actions that had been going on for some time. As early as 1874, the western half of lower Westchester County, having attracted numbers of people who were part of the general progression northward, was joined to New York as the so-called "Annexed District." By 1898, the steady growth in population and the expansion of commerce, industry and transportation facilities had determined that Greater New York would embrace not only Manhattan and the Bronx (as the former "Annexed District," plus the eastern half of lower Westchester County was named), but also Queens County west of Hempstead, Richmond County (Staten Island) and Kings County (Brooklyn).[55] To many New Yorkers of the time, Brooklyn, Queens, Staten Island and the Bronx were unexplored territory, but to the older immigrants whose economic status had improved, these sections offered the possibility of better housing and healthier surroundings for themselves and their children. The departure of the latter, who were mainly of Irish and German extraction, left openings in the tenements that abounded in Manhattan and which were quickly filled by the newer immigrant groups.

Between 1900 and 1910, the population of New York rose from 3,437,302 to 4,746,833, wireless communication between New York and England had been made possible by Marconi, and the Wright brothers had constructed a plane that could fly over New York harbor. However, a proposed child labor law was defeated because limiting a child's working hours was considered an infringment on his liberty.[56] The twentieth century also saw a growing interest in women's rights, one phase of which, woman suffrage, caused considerable controversy while enlisting support from women of all ranks of society. When, in 1912, Mrs. O.H.P. Belmont, the former Alva Vanderbilt then nearing her sixtieth birthday, marshaled a long parade down Fifth Avenue from Fifty-ninth Street to Washington Square, the feminist marchers included socialites, businesswomen, trade unionists, factory workers and housewives. The suffrage battle continued until, following the passage of the Nineteenth Amendment, women finally went to the polls in 1920. Meanwhile, however, with the entrance of the United States into the first World War in 1917 and the organization of the National League for Woman's Service, women replaced absent men in business offices, banks, department stores and factories, as well as filling positions in the many wartime agencies set up by the Federal Government.[57]

After the war in Europe ended, all New York turned out to welcome their own regiments—the 27th Division and the Fighting 69th—as they marched up Fifth Avenue, where later in September, 1919, the grand victory parade led by General John J. Pershing attracted dense crowds and a shower of ticker tape. However, attention was soon turned to domestic problems as a wave of strikes spread through the country and the resulting general unrest worsened when a group of anarchists used bombs to further their cause, one of which exploded amidst the dense noonday crowd on Wall Street on September 16, 1920, killing thirty-eight persons.[58]

Passage of the Prohibition Amendment triggered further social change, as the familiar New York corner saloon and the more elegant hotel or club bar were outlawed, to be replaced by the "speakeasy," or illegal saloon, and the advent of a new kind of criminal, the bootlegger.

In the midtown area, many an available brownstone house with a basement entrance was transformed into a nightclub, one of which, the Twenty-one Club, was internationally famous. It offered an atmosphere of aristocratic elegance, while its electrically controlled devices could, in the event of a raid, protect its patrons by making strategic sections of wall turn to cover incriminating evidence. In time, many of these establishments were dominated by a growing class of gangsters and racketeers, some of whom would receive the protection of such New York politicians as Manhattan's powerful Tammany district leader, James T. Hines, who protected, among others, mobsters Arthur (Dutch Schultz) Flegenheimer and Salvatore (Charles "Lucky" Luciano) Lucania.[59]

The Twenties, bringing the restrictive immigration legislation of 1921 and 1924 which reduced the pressure for housing, especially in the slum areas of the city, also saw the continuing movement north of midtown's wealthy residents. By 1925, as tax assessments grew exorbitantly high[60] and the earlier bountiful supply of Irish and other ethnic servants diminished, the private homes of the wealthy gave way before the encroaching tide of commerce. Even the Vanderbilts were impelled to move uptown, some even taking apartments. Such a departure from the earlier tradition that a home had to be a private dwelling had been made acceptable by the availability of buildings such as The Dakota at 1 West 72nd Street and, later, 998 Fifth Avenue on the northwest corner of 81st Street. When the latter was built in 1911, ninety percent of fashionable New York society lived in private homes; twenty-five years later, ninety percent of fashionable New York would be living in apartment houses, with much of the change due to the kind of quality inspired by the builders of 998 Fifth Avenue. Abandoning the "upstairs-downstairs" concept, the builders had provided six to nine servants' rooms per apartment in the back, with the front part for the family . The largest apartment, twenty-five rooms, was rented by Murray Guggenheim for $25,000 per year; the second largest, about twenty rooms, went to Senator Elihu Root for $15,000 a year.[61]

By 1925, the revival of the Ku Klux Klan, founded in Georgia in 1915, had brought on an upsurge of violence, with the most virulent attacks now directed against Catholics and Jews, who were depicted as dangerous enemies of the old America. Nevertheless, at the Democratic Convention of 1928 in Houston, Texas, a Catholic, New York-born Alfred E. Smith, who had served in the New York State Assembly for years before being elected Governor of New York in 1918 and again in 1922, 1924 and 1926, received the nomination for the presidency on the first ballot. In the ensuing campaign, the vicious invective directed against Smith was dealt with reasonably as he attempted logically to show that Catholics faced no conflict of loyalties between their religious and political obligations. When it proved to no avail, Smith, although distressed by the manner of his defeat, nevertheless accepted the outcome gallantly and calmly.[62] Less than a year later, the country's era of prosperity ended when the stock market crashed on October 24, 1929. The resulting panic that gripped the city spread throughout the nation, as banks failed and bread lines and apple-sellers became common sights on street corners. So deep was the ensuing depression that, despite all the New Deal legislation of President Franklin Delano Roosevelt's administration, widespread unemployment persisted right up to the years of World War II. Inevitably, the cathedral, as well as its parishioners, felt the repercussions of the events of these years and the changes associated with them.

CHAPTER V

The War Years
Michael J. Lavelle (continued)
and Bishop Joseph F. Flannelly
(1939-1969)

During the more than three decades following the dedication and opening of the cathedral many improvements had been made to carry out the original design, among which the completion of the two spires (1888) and the installation of the bells in the northern one (1897), as well as the construction of the Lady Chapel (1901-06) had proved very costly. As early as 1900, Archbishop Corrigan had expressed the desire to have the consecration of the cathedral take place in May 1904, the twenty-fifth anniversary of its opening. To this end, he wrote to the trustees, urging the "curtailing of all expenses, as much as possible, in order to devote whatever can be spared to the paying of the debt."[1] Corrigan, however, was not destined to see the realization of his plans and his sudden death in 1902 left their completion to his successor John Farley. Because the time and money required for the development and execution of plans that would insure the perfect harmonization of the proposed Lady Chapel with the overall architectural beauty of the cathedral far exceeded the original estimates, the first Mass was not offered there until December 1906.

By 1910, when Farley began to make plans for the consecration, the mortgage on the cathedral had grown to

$850,000, an amount the archbishop was determined to pay in full. Accordingly, he advised the trustees that he planned to raise the sum of $450,000 from individual and parish contributions, and requested the board to take such action as might be necessary "to borrow on the credit of the trustees, the remaining sum of $400,000."[2] With the success of these efforts, the cathedral mortage was cleared, an accomplishment which the trustees gracefully acknowledged was due largely to "the contributions of the faithful of the archdiocese, inspired by His Grace, the Most Reverend Archbishop of New York." Recalling the humble origins of the Catholics of New York when the cathedral was begun, the trustees declared "Our Archbishop had guided his Church to its present fruitfulness, and to him will come the reward from unborn millions when they realize his work and bring to a more perfect development what he has so well done."[3]

The solemn consecration of St. Patrick's to the service of God on October 5, 1910, marked another milestone in the history of this preeminent cathedral which serves both as mother church of an important archdiocese and parish church in the great and ever-changing Empire City. As the church in which the archbishop exercises his ceremonial functions, St. Patrick's has been the setting for countless liturgical ceremonies and celebrations marking significant events, both current and historical, associated with the archdiocese. Since a full account of this aspect of the cathedral's storied past properly belongs in a history of the archdiocese, only passing mention will be made in this work which focuses mainly on the cathedral as parish church. Suffice it to note here that the Fifth Avenue cathedral has witnessed the solemn installation of each of the successors of New York's first two archbishops: Michael Augustine Corrigan (1886-1902), John Murphy Farley (1903-18), Patrick Joseph Hayes (1919-38), Francis Joseph Spellman (1939-67) and Terence J. Cooke (1968-1983). When the last four,

John Cardinal Farley
Archbishop of New York (1903-1918)

in turn, were elected to the College of Cardinals[4] (Farley in 1911, Hayes in 1924, Spellman in 1946 and Cooke in 1969), their return to New York from Rome was, in each case, the occasion for a joyous celebration by non-Catholics as well as Catholics of the city.[5]

The rich liturgical history of the cathedral has also included a wide variety of observances, among others, the annual celebration of the feast of St. Patrick, titular saint of the cathedral; various anniversaries of the archdiocese, diocese and the cathedral itself; ceremonies of ordination of priests and the consecration of bishops; as well as the more sombre occasions associated with the obsequies of members of the hierarchy, clergy and laity, and the special Masses and prayer services offered in times of war and other disasters abroad and at home. Frequently in the case of events of the latter kind, spiritual support has been supplemented by material assistance for the victims, as was the case, to cite just one example, when more than $62,000 was sent to aid those in distress following the April 1906 earthquake in San Francisco. Some $20,000 of this amount was collected by a lay committee appointed by Farley, while the remainder came from the Catholic churches of the archdiocese.[6]

For Americans of the twentieth century, a peaceful life has become an increasingly rare commodity as United States citizens became involved in such cataclysmic events as two World Wars, as well as those in Korea, Vietnam and, more recently, the violent eruptions in such countries as Iran and El Salvador. Moreover, at home the never-ending escalation of domestic violence has been experienced to varying degrees by every sector of our society, including the churches. While the cathedral has not suffered anything like the kind of damage inflicted upon some of the city's Jewish synagogues in recent times, neither has it entirely escaped. During the years before this country's entrance into World War I, among the citizens who were angered by President

Woodrow Wilson's neutral policy there were those whose feelings found expression in violent acts of one kind or another. Although never clearly established, it seems likely that it was some of the latter who were responsible for the bomb which exploded in St. Patrick's a few days after Cardinal Farley, at his Mass there on October 4, 1914, had spoken in support of peace. Fortunately, the explosion occurred at a time when no service was in progress and, providentially, the few people who were in the cathedral suffered no injuries.[7] The following May, precautions were taken when it was learned that two anarchists planned to set off a bomb during the 7:30 A.M. Mass, usually a well attended service. Happily, before any damage was done, two detectives stationed in the cathedral and dressed as cleaning women apprehended the criminals who subsequently received prison sentences.

With the entrance of the United States into the war in April 1917, consideration was given to the question of "war or bomb insurance" on the cathedral, but the trustees decided "it was unnecessary at the present time."[8] As the men of cathedral parish were swept up in the national spirit of patriotism they, along with their fellow Catholics and other citizens of different persuasions across the land, through conscription and voluntary enlistments increased the fighting forces of the country from 378,000 in April 1917 to 4,700,000 in November 1918. Although the government kept no records of the religious affiliations of the men in the armed forces, it has been estimated that of the total Catholic population of 17,549,324 in the United States in 1918, some 804,569 served in the war, of whom 22,552 died.[9] Among these, not all were killed in action for the worldwide influenza epidemic of 1918-19, the worst in history, took an estimated 20,000,000 lives, including 548,000 in the United States alone. Out of a total population of 3,215,879 in New York City, deaths from the flu or resulting pneumonia between September 1918 and March 1919 reached 33,387, with the highest incidence of mortality in the 21-29 year old group.[10] Of the 64,600 enlisted men from the Archdiocese of New York, some 1,310 lost their lives.[11]

While the world was at war, news of the death of Cardinal Farley on September 17, 1918, after a short illness caused further shock and sorrow to Catholics and non-Catholics of New York and others throughout the country. The cathedral trustees in recording "their inexpressible sorrow"at the loss of their "president, Cardinal Archbishop and friend" declared that "his achievements in the material and spiritual spheres of his activities are too many to be noted...and too well known to require recital." Among his many outstanding qualities they cited his "piety, wisdom, executive powers, gentleness, firmness, human sympathy and love of country," which although now "lost to his flock and to his country as a living force" would survive in their memory as an inspiration to higher things.[12] After the Mass of Requiem in the cathedral at which the aged Cardinal of Baltimore, James Gibbons, was present, the mortal remains of the fourth Archbishop of New York were placed in the crypt alongside those of his predecessors and his red hat was hung high in the sanctuary.

During the war, Catholic and non-Catholic women worked at home, making surgical supplies, setting up canteens to feed soldiers enroute to the camps, and assisting with clerical work and social and welfare programs. Leadership in these efforts included a number of New York Catholics such as Teresa O'Donohue, President of the League of Catholic Women,[13] who also served as a member of the Mayor's Committee of Women on National Defense Work, and Mrs. Nicholas Brady, one of the vice-chairwomen of New York State's Women's Committee of the Council of National Defense.[14] With the formation of the National Catholic War Council (NCWC) in August 1917, a unified

and coordinated plan of action among all Catholic organizations was developed to deal with what Cardinal Gibbons
called "the severest test, not only of our spirit of zeal, but our
ability to organize and to cope with new difficulties."[15]
Among the latter, the shortage of Catholic chaplains was so
serious that when war was declared in 1917, there was only
one chaplain for every 3,500 men. However, following the
appointment of Bishop Hayes as military ordinary in
November 1917, the number of Catholic chaplains rapidly
increased and when the Armistice was signed on November
11, 1918, there were over 1,000 Catholic chaplains in active
duty and an additional 500 volunteers on call.[16]

In the decade following the cessation of the war, the
country's rising tide of prosperity was enjoyed in varying
degrees by New Yorkers, including those of the cathedral
parish. As the city's growing commercial interests provided
more job opportunities for men in the expanding fields of
white-collar positions and high-skilled manual occupations,
there was also a notable decline in the low-paying domestic
and personal service type jobs, usually filled by women. The
latter, now better educated and trained, were shifting over
to higher paying clerical and professional positions.[17]
Moreoever, speculation on the Stock Exchange during
these years was not limited to the wealthy, as a runaway bull
market attracted middle-class teachers, shop-keepers,
clerks, taxi-drivers and a host of others who bought stocks
on margin believing they had found the portal to riches.
Until the stock market crash of October 24, 1929, and the
ensuing panic that spread throughout the country, New
Yorkers, as well as large numbers of their fellow citizens,
believed that the great American dream of becoming rich
was rapidly being realized.

While these good times lasted, some were moved to
greater generosity in the support of their church. Over the
years, the trustees of St. Patrick's had repeatedly urged

Monsignor Lavelle to find ways to increase the revenues of the cathedral.[18] Not until 1919, however, did Lavelle institute, in addition to the ordinary Sunday collection, two envelope collections a year, one on the first Sunday of Lent and the second on the last Sunday of November. A Board of Help was also organized to persuade the people of the need to support their church, "encouraging generosity and lending any other assistance within their will and power."[19] Tangible evidence of the parishioners' ability and willingness to support the cathedral was soon forthcoming. During the 1920's, as the cathedral's yearly expenses increased from some $84,375 in 1920 to almost $190,000 by 1928, the rector's financial reports for five of these years showed a small surplus.[20] No doubt this was due in large part to Lavelle's regular reminders to his people that the cathedral was dependent upon their voluntary offerings to meet expenses connected with the school; the choir; lighting, heating and repairs in the cathedral and school; insurance; salaries for the clergy, teachers, sexton, verger and ushers; contributions to numerous charities; and other contingencies such as that involved in repairing the damage caused when the north spire was struck by lightning in June 1925.[21]

In the rector's letter of February 14, 1926 to his parishioners, Lavelle noted that in the special collection on the first Sunday of Lent the previous year, about 3,000 envelopes had been returned when, in his opinion, it might easily have been 5,000. Addressing "these other 2,000," he urged them to "make the smallest offering $5. Double it if you can. Other contributions can run according to ability up to $1000," adding a reminder to his flock that the priests "take up this collection ourselves to show our deep interest in what concerns you so much."[22] If the ordinary maintenance of the cathedral was costly, the expense connected with the Cathedral Improvement Program launched by Cardinal Hayes in anticipation of the Golden Jubilee of St. Patrick's in 1929 called for even more generous support from all New York Catholics.

As early as 1924, Hayes suggested that the trustees begin to make plans for raising the funds needed to carry out the contemplated repairs and improvements.[23] The latter included extensive alterations of the sanctuary which was to be lengthened and paved with gray and green marble, inlaid with mosaic symbols. The refurbishments planned embraced a new archbishop's throne, a sanctuary screen of Gothic design, sedilia for the clergy, a marble communion rail with a center bronze gate and new ventilating and lighting systems. Other projected improvements included stained glass windows for the Lady Chapel, reconstruction of the choir gallery and the installation of a new chancel organ, bronze doors to replace the oak ones of the main portal and a pamphlet rack.[24] When, in 1926, the proposed cathedral improvements began to receive publicity in the local papers, fund-raising efforts were stepped up, one of which, Lavelle's Sunday Dollar Club, had yielded $128,500 by December 1929.[25]

Despite the good progress made on the work of repairing and improving the cathedral, it was deemed advisable to postpone the date for the celebration of the 50th anniversary of its dedication to May 25, 1930, in order that as much of the restoration as possible might be completed. Even so, some items such as the bronze doors had to be left for future implementation because of the great expense involved. The depressed state of the economy during the 1930's made it difficult, if not impossible, for many of the cathedral's supporters to continue their generous contributions.[26] Thus it was Hayes' successor, Cardinal Spellman, who not only directed that the unfinished work be completed, but also initiated many additional renovations and improvements of the cathedral during his more than twenty-eight years in New York.

Although the anniversary celebration of the cathedral was postponed, plans for the observance of Monsignor Lavelle's golden jubilee of ordination were under way early in 1929 when the Board of Diocesan Consultors invited about one hundred pastors to a meeting at the Chancery Office to arrange a fitting testimonial for the jubilarian.[27] The program planned was to include a Solemn Mass at 11:00 A.M. on June 5, 1929, at which Lavelle would be celebrant and Cardinal Hayes would preside. In anticipation of this event, Hayes wrote to Rome in March requesting that the honor of prothonotary apostolic be bestowed upon Lavelle. No response was received until May 7th, when a cablegram arrived conveying only the Holy Father's apostolic blessing upon Lavelle. When Hayes sought an explanation through the good offices of the Rector of the North American College, Eugene S. Burke, he learned that the Vatican claimed it had never received his March letter. Fortunately, all was well when on June 4th a radiogram reached Hayes from Rome stating that the Holy Father had named Lavelle "Prothonotary Apostolic Ad Instar Participanitium."[29] Thus, when the jubilarian appeared the following morning for Mass, the cardinal invested him with the miter, ring and pectoral cross--pontificals which his new title permitted him to wear four times a year during a pontifical Mass.[29]

After the Mass, a buffet luncheon was served in Cathedral College so as to afford everyone an opportunity, in an informal setting, to offer personal congratulations to Lavelle. Some days later, on the evening of June 10th, the Board of Trustees sponsored a testimonial banquet in the Hotel Biltmore at which the cardinal thanked the rector for his "devoted, fruitful and brilliant ministry" and expressed the wish that "many more blessed years. . . be granted to the prelate and pastor, whose illustrious name is so happily and intimately associated with our majestic Cathedral."

Patrick Cardinal Hayes
Archbishop of New York (1919-1938)

Lavelle's gratitude for the entire festivities was warmly expressed in a letter to Hayes in which the rector stated "the beauty and magnitude of it all would have been impossible without your powerful impulse." Although he felt he did not deserve such kindness, Lavelle added "it would be an inspiration to better efforts" in the future and render him "entirely at your service for whatever may tend to promote the success of your administration and your own personal happiness."[30]

During the sixty years of Lavelle's priestly life all of which were spent at his beloved cathedral, fifty-two of them as its rector, he became an increasingly well known figure beyond the parish. His reputation as preacher, lecturer and administrator gradually spread throughout New York City, the archdiocese and beyond, involving him in the work of countless religious, educational and social committees, federations and associations. Interested in all levels of education from elementary school to university, Lavelle in 1909 was recommended by the trustees of The Catholic University of America as one of three possible candidates for the university rectorship to succeed Bishop Denis J. O'Connell whose administration spanned the years from 1903-09. When the appointment went to Thomas J. Shahan, professor of church history and patrology at the university since 1891 who had received three more votes than Lavelle on the *terna* sent to Rome,[31] the latter was left to continue his ministry in New York. Under five successive archbishops of New York, Lavelle worked ceaselessly for the cathedral and his parishioners, also assuming the duties of vicar general from 1902-19 under Cardinal Farley and again from 1934-39 under Cardinals Patrick Hayes and Francis Spellman.

In his role as pastor, Lavelle on occasion addressed a circular letter to his parishoners, reminding them that parochial revenues were not sufficient to meet current expenses and urging them to greater generosity in order to make the cathedral self-supporting.[32] Another time the letter would dwell on the "evils abroad"and offer advice on the ways to combat them. In one such communication, Lavelle outlined what he considered the "proper way to spend the summer months," including the frequent use of the sacraments and fidelity, punctuality and devotion in attending Mass. Referring to the times as "pernicious," the rector asserted that the Catholic antidote for "this poison" might be found in "pious and elevated reading" and he urged his flock to "patronize Catholic newspapers, magazines and literature in general."[33] With the launching of the *Cathedral Bulletin* in 1922, Lavelle and his successors in the rectorship had direct access to a monthly publication of their own through which to inform, instruct and admonish the members of the parish. As might be expected, each incumbent up to the present has exhibited a style of communication reflective not only of the individual's personality, but also of the Catholic climate of the time with, not surprisingly, Lavelle's appearing the most paternalistic and authoritarian.

Lavelle, who enjoyed a wide reputation as an eloquent preacher and was much in demand as a speaker at educational, social and other gatherings, adopted a very forthright style for his annual letter to the parishioners of the cathedral. This communication, designed to remind his people of the special envelope collection to be taken up on the first Sunday of Lent at all Masses in the cathedral, varied in composition very little from year to year, containing an odd mixture of financial information, pious comments and thinly veiled demands which his readers apparently found unexceptional. During the 'twenties, while both income and expenditures showed increases, the surplus was never large after all operating expenses were taken care of, so Lavelle strongly urged his people to greater generosity so that they might "feel they have purchased a right to kneel in God's temple..."[34] With the advent of hard times in the 'thirties, Lavelle's letter of February 15, 1931 reported that, in addition to a decrease in the amount received for operating expenses during 1930, there was also a sharp decline in contributions to the Jubilee Improvement Fund. Declaring that bills must be paid whether "the sun shines or the skies be cloudy," he reminded them that... "not a child is taught there is a God in heaven, nor a sacrament administered, nor a Mass celebrated without entailing expense that must be met in this Cathedral by the people who worship within its walls and who enjoy its spiritual benefits." He then urged them "to sanctify Lent in its very beginning," adding "every adult person will...present his contribution next Sunday...proportionate to the means God has given him. The clergy of the Cathedral, with me at their head, will take your offerings ourselves."[35]

Meanwhile, during the decade following Lavelle's celebration of his golden jubilee and, a year later, the observance of the fiftieth anniversary of the opening of St. Patrick's, New Yorkers and, indeed, the majority of Americans faced uneasy times. In the city, stores and offices stood empty, the number of unemployed mounted, long bread lines multiplied and shanties again sprang up in Central Park and along the Hudson River near the railroad tracks. Not until the years of World War II was there a sufficient number of job opportunities for the employment of practically all the employable labor force.[36] However, despite the depression, expensive land on Fifth Avenue became the sites selected for the erection of the tall buildings that today tower over the spires of St. Patrick's, forming part of the most famous skyline in the world. The Empire State Building at 34th Street and Fifth Avenue, as completed in 1931, was a modified version of the original design, thinned to a tall shaft to cut costs. Rockefeller Center also began taking shape in that troubled period when, in 1930, the work of wrecking and excavation began. During the ensuing years, as Fifth Avenue enjoyed a worldwide reputation as the main shopping center, with large department stores entrenched on the stretch from 34th Street north, and with specialty shops, luxury hotels and a host of business concerns slowly pushing out many of the remaining residents, the changes in mid-Manhattan appeared irreversible.

During the three decades from 1900-1930, the population of the New York Metropolitan Region grew one hundred and eleven per cent, as compared with the sixty-two percent increase in the national figure. However, in Manhattan where the very rich traditionally have maintained homes close to the center of things, the number of areas containing the homes of the very rich and the very poor increased between 1900 and 1930, even though, beginning in 1920, the population of Manhattan as a whole began to decline. The flight of the middle class from Manhattan from 1920 on brought increasing numbers first to nearby areas such as the Bronx, Queens and southern Westchester, and by the 1950's, farther away to Suffolk County on Long Island and to Monmouth, Middlesex, Somerset and Morris Counties in New Jersey.[37] Various estimates indicate that between 1950-1960 the central core of New York City lost about a million members of the middle class. Moreover, by the 1960's, the attractiveness of Park Avenue which, following the covering over of the railroad tracks, had replaced Fifth Avenue as the locale of elegant homes, was being invaded by commercialism on the stretch between 42nd and 59th streets. There, new office buildings, designed according to the current vogue for steel and glass, were replacing the stone buildings of the past.[38]

By the time Lavelle celebrated his 80th birthday in the spring of 1936, a number of the changes cited above were still in the future, although the threat to world peace posed by the rise to power of Adolf Hitler in Germany had by that

year become so ominous that innumerable prayers had
already been offered by the many alarmed people of Europe
and the United States. Nevertheless, the rector's birthday
was a happy one, enhanced by the felicitations he received
from Pope Pius XI, and by the Mass in the cathedral at
which Cardinal Hayes presided and offered thanks to God
for the cathedral and its rector, noting that the two were so
close in their service of God and country as to bring many
blessings to the city.[39] Moreover, the following November,
the observance of the 26th anniversary of the consecration
of the cathedral became a never-to-be-forgotten occasion by
reason of the presence of Cardinal Eugenio Pacelli, then
Secretary of State and later Pope Pius XII, who had just
completed a tour of the United States by air, accompanied
by the then Auxiliary Bishop of Boston, Francis Spellman
who had also arranged the itinerary. When Pacelli left for
Rome, those riding to the pier with him included Cardinal
Hayes and Monsignor Lavelle.[40]

Two years later, on September 4th, the news of the death
of Cardinal Hayes who had passed away in his sleep at a
summer villa in Monticello after some five years of failing
health saddened not only his many close friends such as
Lavelle, but also Catholics and non-Catholics far and wide
who had known him as the "Cardinal of Charities." When
the hearse carrying the remains of the cardinal approached
the cathedral, the great bells in the high tower tolled a sad,
slow dirge while inside the black and purple draped edifice,
Lavelle and some five hundred priests were among those
gathered to offer tribute and to pray for him who for more
than nineteen years had been their archbishop, fourteen of
them as a cardinal. Following the prayers offered in the
cathedral, the body was taken to the parlor of the archiepiscopal residence on Madison Avenue and the next day,
white-mitred and red-slippered with a rosary twined around
the lifeless hands, was returned to the cathedral to lie in state

before the high altar. Of the thousands who passed by the bier and later filled the cathedral for the solemn obsequies, many faces showed the sorrow they were feeling. Among the three cardinals, twelve archbishops and fifty-five bishops present were two former New Yorkers who had known Hayes since their boyhood: Cardinal George Mundelein of Chicago who celebrated the Mass of Requiem and Archbishop Joseph Rummel of New Orleans who gave the eulogy. After the final absolution, interment was in the crypt near the tombs of Cardinal Farley and Archbishop Corrigan under whom Hayes had served, and not far from those of Cardinal McCloskey and Archbishop Hughes. Some days later another red hat was added to the two hanging high above the sanctuary of St. Patrick's.[41]

To serve as administrator of the archdiocese during the months that New York awaited the naming of a successor to Hayes, the consultors chose, with Rome's approval, Stephen J. Donahue, a native of New York whom Hayes had consecrated Auxiliary Bishop of New York and Titular Bishop of Medea in 1934. As might be expected, speculation about possible candidates for the vacancy had abounded for some time when the unexpected death of Pius XI early in 1939 and the subsequent election of Eugenio Pacelli as Pius XII added another factor to the discussions. Finally, on April 24th, the news came over the radio from Rome that the new pope had appointed Francis Spellman Archbishop of New York. Speaking in the name of the priests, religious and laity of the archdiocese, Donahue lost no time in pledging their "loyalty and obedience" to the archbishop-elect, promising to "pray for his health, strength and every blessing to carry on the great burden that has been placed upon his shoulders." On his part, Spellman had already assured his flock-to-be that he knew he could rely upon "those whom Cardinal Hayes has guided...to guide me," adding that he would count also on the cooperation of "my friend down through the years, Bishop Donahue...and the enlightened counsel of the venerable and beloved Vicar General, Monsignor Lavelle."[42]

It was as Vicar General that Lavelle on May 23rd at the installation ceremony in the cathedral read the papal bulls addressed in turn to the new archbishop, the clergy and laity of the City and Archdiocese of New York, and finally to the "Bishops Suffragan to the Metropolitan Church of New York." In his response, Archbishop Spellman recalled his visits to St. Patrick's during the years he was a student at Fordham University and, in 1916, after his return from the North American College in Rome, when he offered his first Mass in America at the altar of the cathedral's Lady Chapel. After paying tribute to his predecessor, Cardinal Hayes, he referred to Pius XII and his visit to New York when he was Papal Secretary of State, adding "I have been assigned to this work by the Supreme Pastor of Christendom [and] affirm that all my life's energies will be spent...in the gaining of souls for Christ."

In addition to the presiding prelate, Amleto G. Cicognani, Apostolic Delegate to the United States, and Bishop Donahue who was celebrant of the Solemn Pontifical Mass which followed, nearly half of the American hierarchy were present for this occasion together with countless monsignori, priests, brothers and seminarians. Missing was Boston's Cardinal William O'Connell whose health did not permit him to attend, but who was represented by three of Boston's monsignori, one of whom was the future Cardinal Richard Cushing. An estimated 5,000 people reportedly filled the cathedral, while outside still greater numbers overflowed into the nearby streets. Equally large numbers turned up the following evening for the public reception held in the Hotel Commodore where former Governor Alfred E. Smith welcomed the new archbishop on behalf of the Catholic men's organizations of the city, while Lady

Armstrong spoke for the women of the archdiocese and Bishop Donahue pledged the fealty of the priests and religious of New York.[43]

The following month Archbishop Spellman presided and Lavelle pontificated (a privilege his rank as prothonotary apostolic accorded him) at the Jubilee Mass in the cathedral in celebration of the 60th anniversary of the rector's ordination. The many tributes paid to Lavelle that evening at the dinner in his honor at the Hotel Commodore included a cablegram from Pius XII conferring his apostolic benediction; a letter of congratulations from the Apostolic Delegate, Archbishop Cicognani; a personal letter of felicitation from President Franklin D. Roosevelt and a scroll from the Mayor of New York City testifying to his "distinguished and exceptional public service." Three years earlier, Lavelle had remarked to a friend that he planned to retire in a few years and would then write his memoirs.[44] Now in his 84th year, this anniversary festivity proved to be the last public function at which he would be present. The following day he was confined to his bed and, except for a few short automobile rides, he never again left the rectory. Four months later, on October 7, unable to attend the Solemn Pontifical Mass offered in commemoration of the 29th anniversary of the consecration of St. Patrick's, the message Lavelle sent was simple: "Tell the people that my prayers are always with them and with the Cathedral."[45]

Ten days later, at 8:34 P.M. in his room in the rectory the venerable second rector of the cathedral breathed his last. At his bedside were the archbishop, two of the cathedral priests, two doctors and Lavelle's two sisters. In a statement issued later that evening, Archbishop Spellman expressed his feeling of personal loss and sorrow, adding "even to the very end I sought, received and followed his counsel." A few days earlier, after Lavelle had asked for and received the archbishop's absolution and blessing, Spellman had confided his intention to have the rector's mortal remains placed in the crypt of the cathedral, news which brought a "smile of joy and gratitude" to the face of the faithful servant of New York's mother church.[46] As soon as the news of the rector's death spread, tributes to him arrived from near and far, from the great and those of less consequence in the eyes of the world. The Reverend Henry F. Hammer, who had served for twenty years (1917-37) under Lavelle at the cathedral, believed the latter had "done more to promote understanding and good feeling toward Catholic religion on the part of non-Catholics than any other man of his time" by "spanning the religious life of our city like a modern Colossus... with a great human heart, a brilliant and keen intellect..."[47] Another New Yorker, John Joseph Mitty, then Archbishop of San Francisco, noted that the Church in New York "owes much to his [Lavelle's] wisdom, zeal and untiring energy," adding "New York will miss the colorful character, the ready sympathy and heartfelt loyalty of Monsignor Lavelle." To Governor Alfred E. Smith, Lavelle's charity "knew no bounds."[48]

After the thousands, known and unknown, had passed the bier which was moved from the rectory to the cathedral Thursday afternoon, a Mass of Requiem offered at 9:00 the following morning was, very fittingly, attended by all the children of Cathedral School. That evening, after Divine Office had been chanted by the priests of the archdiocese, the casket was closed, not to be reopened. The next morning immediately following the Pontifical Mass of Requiem celebrated by the archbishop, interment was in the crypt, a part of St. Patrick's Lavelle undoubtedly had visited regularly during his sixty years of active service there, with never a thought that he himself would one day be laid to rest near the archbishops he had served and in the cathedral he had cherished.

The Reverend Joseph F. Flannelly, chosen as Lavelle's

Bishop Joseph Flannelly

successor, had been born on West 51st Street in the city and was the first graduate of Blessed Sacrament School to be ordained a priest and, later, consecrated a bishop. Upon completion of his studies at St. Joseph's Seminary, Dunwoodie, he was ordained in 1918 and subsequently served for twenty years at Our Lady of the Rosary in Yonkers, where he supervised the parish school and taught singing to the school choir.[49] Then in 1938 he was appointed senior assistant at the cathedral and, following Lavelle's death, was named administrator. After being honored as papal chamberlain in 1941 and domestic prelate in April 1943, Flannelly, on December 16, 1948, was consecrated Titular Bishop of Medea and Auxiliary Bishop of New York, one of the record number of twenty-four priests who were raised to the episcopate in the cathedral during the first twenty years of Cardinal Spellman's ministry in New York.[50] On Christmas Day, the new bishop celebrated his first Pontifical Mass in St. Patrick's.

During Lavelle's rectorship, as the population of midtown expanded and new parishes were established east of Third Avenue and north of 42nd Street, the parochial district originally assigned to the catheral parish had shrunk to the area extending from 44th to 59th Streets, Third Avenue to Seventh Avenue. Although no further contraction of St. Patrick's parish boundaries occurred, the thirty years of Flannelly's administration witnessed radical changes throughout this section of the city, altering the nature of the cathedral's parochial mission and, increasingly, expanding the cathedral's role as an archdiocesan religious center. Nevertheless, the maintenance and improvement of the cathedral itself remained a constant concern of each of the successive archbishops and rectors down to the present. As early as 1939, Spellman had announced plans for the further repairing and remodeling of the cathedral, including a more suitable high altar as well as a new altar for the Lady Chapel.

Chosen by McCloskey, the existing high altar had been appropriate for the original structure with its flat east wall. However, with the completion of the Lady Chapel in 1904, this altar obstructed the vista of the long nave, blocking a view of the Lady Chapel. Upon learning of the proposal to replace the original high altar, Lavelle had declared that it would be done over his dead body.[51] And so it was, for when the new altar of Tavernelle Marble, with its high baldachin of ornate bronze supported by four piers, was completed in 1942 the crypt in which Lavelle had been buried was directly below. Other improvements included the installation of five new stained glass apsidal windows which were unveiled before the new altar below was consecrated by the archbishop on May 9th.[52] The celebrant of the first Mass offered there on May 13th was the Reverend William J. B. Daly who had served as assistant (1886-1902) under the first two rectors of St. Patrick's and who, in 1942, was the oldest living priest associated with the cathedral.[53] A month earlier, Mass had been offered for the first time on the new, smaller altar in the Lady Chapel, where a pure white statue depicting Mary praying with arms extended surmounted the Tavernelle marble altar. The frontal, richly inlaid with colored marble of many shades, was designed to represent the Annunciation.[54]

Meanwhile, the war in Europe, touched off by Hitler's invasion of Poland in the fall of 1939, had effected the surrender of France, leaving only Great Britain to withstand the forces of Hitler and his then ally, Italy's Fascist Benito Mussolini. In the United States, where the main issues of the presidential campaign of 1940 were isolationism versus interventionism, Franklin Delano Roosevelt, whom the nation had elected to the presidency in 1932 when the only issue of consequence was the deepening economic depression, won an unprecedented third term. As a result, continued aid to Great Britain was guaranteed by the Lend-Lease Bill passed in March 1941. However, after the December 7th surprise attack on the United States naval base at Pearl Harbor, Hawaii, by the Japanese who had signed a pact with Germany and Italy in September 1940, Congress declared war on Japan on December 8th, and a few days later against Germany and Italy. Following Pearl Harbor, Spellman lost no time in placing the services of the priests and religious of the archdiocese and all its resources and facilities at the disposition of the federal government. Accordingly, the trustees moved "to comply with the expressed wish of the United States Government to donate all unnecessary railings, fences and markers in the cemetery for...use...in the prosecution of the war."[55]

Not all Catholics of the archdiocese or of cathedral parish

Francis Cardinal Spellman, Archbishop of New York (1939-1967) with Archbishop Angelo Roncalli, later Pope John XXIII, in Istanbul, Turkey, 1943

were as enthusiastic as their archbishop in supporting President Roosevelt's war policies. As one parishioner wrote "this is no time for the Catholic Church or Archbishop Spellman to pusseyfoot on the warmongers...We Catholic mothers are getting out of patience..."[56] In 1942, when the New York *Times* published the nation-wide address made by Spellman under the auspices of the Knights of Columbus which called upon every American to be ready to fight and, if necessary, to die to preserve the democratic way of life,[57] he was advised by a Brooklyn man that the reaction of a prominent professor-friend of his was that "the Archbishop of New York should imitate the Bishop of Brooklyn and keep out of this political mess."[58] Despite such criticism Spellman remained a powerful ally of Roosevelt and by 1942, 53,174 men and women from the archdiocese had joined the ranks of those in the service of their country; two years later, that number had increased to 149,657, and hanging from the choir loft of the cathedral a flag with 1,396 gold stars commemorated those who had died in the war effort.[59]

Another death in October of 1944, that of Alfred E. Smith, four-term Governor of New York and unsuccessful Democratic nominee for the presidency in 1928, occurred while the archbishop was making his second visit to the troops at the front. Upon learning that Smith was near death, Spellman had cabled instructions to insure that his old friend would be accorded the full honors of the Church. Thus, the coffin bearing the remains of the "Happy Warrior" was brought to the cathedral to lie there in state late into the night, as many thousands paid their respects. Such a privilege had been bestowed upon a layman only once before in the history of the cathedral.[60] Later, Spellman would help to perpetuate his friend's memory with the establishment of the Alfred E. Smith Memorial Foundation, Inc., with its annual dinner, the proceeds of which have made possible the expansion of the many services offered at St. Vincent's Hospital.

Less than three months after the beginning of Roosevelt's fourth term as president and shortly after his return from the Yalta Conference with Winston Churchill and the Russian dictator Joseph Stalin, news of the president's sudden death in Warm Springs, Georgia, shocked the nation and the world. In New York, Spellman wired his condolences to the president's widow and presided at the Votive Mass for the nation offered in the cathedral by Monsignor Flannelly, at which Auxiliary Bishop J. Francis McIntyre read the statement issued by President Harry S Truman calling for national prayer and church attendance on the day of his predecessor's funeral. McIntyre also read a cable from Pius XII expressing a "profound sense of grief born of the high esteem in which we held this renowned statesman and of the friendly relations which he fostered and maintained with the

Holy See." To his condolences, the pontiff added the assurance of prayers for the entire American people and for their new president.[61]

Following the end of the fighting in Europe and Japan there were no parades of celebration on Fifth Avenue as the members of our armed forces returned, for new and more sober issues faced a world which had for a period of years devoted the major portion of its capabilities to destruction and now looked to a future threatened by atomic annihilation. However, both V-E and V-J days, as they were called, brought throngs of people to St. Patrick's for prayers of thanksgiving and the singing of the *Te Deum*, as church bells throughout the city rang and ship and factory whistles joined in concert. There was rejoicing also at the Cathedral Canteen, then located on 51st Street and Madison Avenue, where alumnae of Cathedral High School had helped many of the thousands of servicemen who came to New York during the war to enjoy brief interludes of relaxation, serving them free refreshments and providing dancing partners for them. When the canteen, later known as Cardinal Spellman's Servicemen's Club, moved first to Lexington Avenue at 54th Street, and in 1960 to 487 Park Avenue, everything was still provided without cost to the service personnel who continued to patronize the club. In recognition of this contribution to the welfare of the men and women in the services, General Lyman L. Lemnitzer, Acting Chief of Staff of the Army, at a dinner in the Plaza Hotel on the occasion of Spellman's 70th birthday, presented the cardinal with a medal, the highest honor the Department of Defense may confer upon a civilian, in recognition of his "unfailing devotion to the well being and spiritual welfare of the military personnel."[62]

During the postwar years, a new program of renovation of the exterior and improvement of the interior of St. Patrick's was launched, and the trustees were authorized to

borrow up to $2,000,000 "to be used for necessary perma-
nent improvements to the Cathedral, which is a monument
to, and services the entire Archdiocese of New York."[63]
Blasting in the area during the erection of the building for
Best & Company at 51st Street and Fifth Avenue during the
summer of 1945 may have helped to loosen the large block
of masonry above the 51st Street entrance to the cathedral
which fell to the pavement below on July 12. The incident,
which caused no injury to passerbys and only minor damage
to the pavement, led to an extensive program of inspection
and renovation.[64] During the subsequent work on the exteri-
or of the three buildings—cathedral, archiepiscopal residence and rectory—which took nearly three years to
complete, there was no interruption of services and visitors
from all parts of the world continued to visit St. Patrick's.

By spring 1948, the exterior repairs and other improvements, such as the installation over the main portal of a new
rose window, had been completed. The design of the latter
had originally been worked out by Renwick and was used by
the current designer, Charles Connick. With the death of the
latter before the work was entirely completed, his associates
finished it precisely as planned. In December of the following year, the cardinal blessed the new bronze doors at the
main portal which were sculptured in Gothic design and
decorated with carved figures; new bronze doors of simpler
design had also been provided for the four tower entrances.
The architect who had supervised this work, Charles D.
Maginnis, in a letter to Spellman expressed delight that the
cardinal was "happy about the new doors," adding, "the
project carried a high challenge...so the process has been
an anxious one." In the end, however, he rejoiced that he
had "contributed another item to the Cathedral which will
be worthy of [the cardinal's] administration..."[65]

Fortunately the cost of these and other improvements
such as the blue windows for the clerestory was met in part

from the bequest of $3,000,000 left by the famous radio personality, Major Bowes, "for the beautification of...the cathedral and/or such charitable or eleemosynary institutions at the discretion of Cardinal Spellman."[66] Among the many other prominent New Yorkers who contributed to the enhancement of St. Patrick's was Nelson A. Rockefeller who wrote to Spellman in June 1952 that "after many years of experimentation with trees...we at Rockefeller Center have found the right ones for Fifth Avenue." Convinced that honey locusts were "the only really disease proof and fume resistant variety of tree," Rockefeller stated that should Spellman "care to have trees in front of the Cathedral...I would consider it a privilege to present them to you."[67] By the following October the trees had been planted and Spellman's letter to his friend and neighbor across the avenue declared "I renew the expression of my gratitude for your thoughtfulness and generosity in this regard."[68]

CHAPTER VI

The Challenge of the Present
The Rectorship of Monsignor
James F. Rigney (1969-   )

During the 1950's, the shape of things to come began to
loom more clearly. As the vogue for steel and glass buildings
which had transformed Park Avenue into a glass-walled
canyon later insinuated itself into the area surrounding St.
Patrick's and Rockefeller Center, hotels and office buildings rose like giant glass blocks around them. Despite this
invasion of commercialism and the continuing loss of its
resident parishioners, the refurbished cathedral had probably never before in its history been as busy a center of
activity. Members of the United Nations attended Mass
there, including on one occasion Andrei Vishinski and
Ambassador Nicolai Novikof, representatives of the Krem-
lin,[1] while countless heads of state and civic leaders from all
parts of the world found their way to St. Patrick's, many of
them after a visit to neighboring Rockefeller Center. When
in 1957, Spellman welcomed the President of Italy, Giovanni Gronchi, it marked the first time a head of the Italian
government had ever visited the United States.[2] Meanwhile,
the long, faithful but unheralded tradition of service on the
part of the cathedral's priests and staff continued uninter-
rupted, albeit with many adjustments to meet the needs of a
changing city and a rapidly growing transient congregation.

Instead of living near their places of work as most New York did in the first decades of the twentieth century, by the 1960's nearly two-and-a-half million people were converging daily to jobs in the central business district of Manhattan, the area south of 59th Street.[3] As a growing number of these office workers began to make the cathedral their weekday parish, Mass schedules were adjusted to accommodate those who wished to attend either before work in the morning, or at the noon break for lunch, or after the close of the workday. Another service which had been under discussion for some time was launched in 1955 with the opening of St. Patrick's Information Center at 31 East 50th Street. Its first director, Father Charles J. McManus, a member of the cathedral staff since 1947, began the work of providing information and instruction to all interested in learning more about the Catholic faith and prayer. Open on weekdays from 10:00 A.M. to 9:00 P.M. and Saturdays from 10:00 A.M. to 3:00 P.M., the center scheduled new instruction classes every six weeks and provided a reading room and a library for browsing. Retreats and days of recollection were added as was a telephone service which soon expanded to about a thousand calls a month, while those coming as individuals or in groups to the center numbered about 900 persons in a year.[4] In late 1957, another member of the rectory staff, Father Francis X. Duffy who had served there since 1951, joined McManus at the center where a small staff of lay helpers had been assisting the director as best they could. In the early 1960's, Duffy became director and was assisted by Father Bernard P. Donachie who had been serving at the cathedral since 1955.[5]

The cathedral's long tradition of arranging Masses for Catholic members of service groups in the city such as the Police and Fire Department personnel was expanded over the years to include, among others, employees of such diverse industries as the Teamsters, Radio and Television

Networks, Continental Can Company, Best and Company, Saks Fifth Avenue, Arnold Constable's, Gimbel's and Bloomingdale's. When in December 1951, the first annual Communion Mass for the New York employees of the United States Department of State was offered in the cathedral by Bishop Flannelly, those attending included the personnel of the Voice of America.[6] At the celebration of the centennial of the laying of the cornerstone of St. Patrick's, August 15, 1959, a total of 30,000 persons assisted at the sixteen Masses offered in the cathedral that day. The ceremonial chair used by Archbishop John Hughes in 1858 had been preserved and was placed in the sanctuary opposite the throne of Cardinal Spellman for the centenary celebration.[7]

In the years following World War II, large numbers of Puerto Rican and other Spanish-speaking Catholics emigrated to New York so that by the 1960's they numbered more than 300,000 from Puerto Rico, as well as another 150,000 from other parts of the world. To serve this population, Cardinal Spellman arranged programs of instruction in Spanish for New York priests and religious and provided funding for seminarians from St. Joseph's, Dunwoodie, to spend their summer vacations serving as lay assistants to pastors in Puerto Rico. At St. Patrick's Cathedral, the feast of St. John the Baptist was set aside for a Pontifical Mass for Spanish-speaking New Yorkers. By the cathedral's centennial year, the list of major Hispanic celebrations observed yearly in St. Patrick's had expanded to include: Our Lady of Altagracia (Dominican Republic), Our Lady of Luján (Argentina, Paraguay, Uruguay), Peru National Day, Our Lady of Caridad del Cobre (Cuba), Dia de la Hispanidad, Our Lady of Divine Providence (Puerto Rico), Haitian Mass, Our Lady of Guadalupe (Mexico), and Panama Day Mass, all of which are very well attended.[8]

Still another service was offered to the constantly shifting population of midtown when the cardinal decided that the first chapel of the cathedral would be established in the area between St. Patrick's and the Church of St. Vincent Ferrer. Thus, a ~~theatre~~ at 59th Street and Park Avenue was purchased in 1957 and subsequently renovated for church use as the Chapel of Saints Faith, Hope and Charity of St. Patrick's Cathedral and placed under the jurisdiction of Bishop Flannelly.[9] Some twenty years later, under Flannelly's successor Monsignor James F. Rigney, the chapel was relocated, again in a renovated theatre on East 58th Street between Lexington and Park Avenues, and dedicated by Spellman's successor, Cardinal Terence Cooke, on December 23, 1978.[10] As in the cathedral, the chapel's Mass schedule is designed to accommodate both residents and those who work in the area. Revisions of the earlier laws regarding the Eucharistic fast, particularly that of Pope Paul VI in 1964, at the close of the third session of Vatican Council II requiring only one hour of abstinence from solid food and all beverages (water excepted), have made it possible for all who so desire to receive Holy Communion at any of the scheduled Masses.[11]

During the first century of the Fifth Avenue St. Patrick's history, its rectory had become the home of approximately one hundred and ten resident curates, twenty-two of whom served there for between ten to twenty-five consecutive years.[12] Supplementing the services provided by the rectory priests were guest preachers for special occasions, such as the lecture series for Lent and Advent. During the early 1900's these included, among others, the popular Jesuit William O'Brien Pardow who became known for his Sunday Lenten sermons. For the Advent series, such respected pulpit orators as Father Thomas Ewing Sherman, S.J., son of the famous Civil War General, William Tecumseh Sherman; and the English Benedictine, Abbot Aidan Gasquet, were among those who also attracted large crowds.[13] Later, Fulton J. Sheen while Professor of Philosophy at The

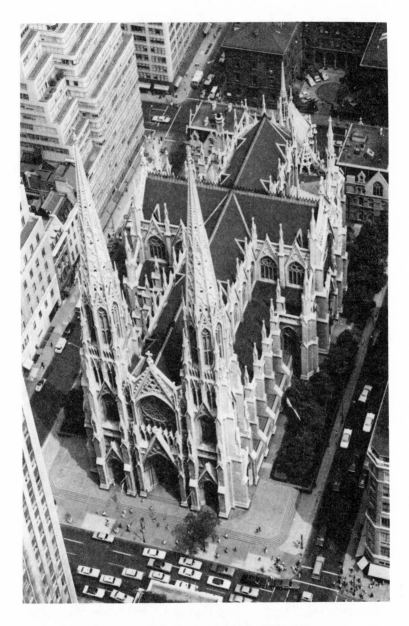

*Aerial view. In right background, the Villard Houses
before erection of Palace Hotel*

Catholic University of America (1926-50) travelled to New York on weekends during many of these years to preach from the cathedral pulpit, drawing throngs of people to his Lenten sermons. Appointed National Director of the Society for the Propagation of the Faith (1950-66) and consecrated Titular Bishop of Caesariana (1951), Bishop Sheen continued to preach at St. Patrick's on special occasions such as Christmas Midnight Mass, the annual "Red Mass" for the lawyers of the archdiocese, etc.

Named Archbishop of the Titular See of Newport, Wales, in 1966, Sheen was singularly honored when, on October 2, 1979, he was singled out for a warm embrace by Pope John Paul II in the sanctuary of St. Patrick's on the occasion of the pope's pastoral visit to the Church of New York. During the sustained applause of those crowded into the cathedral, the pontiff commended the archbishop for having been "a loyal son of the Church" who had "written and spoken well of the Lord Jesus."[14] Two months later, following the death of the eighty-four-year-old archbishop on December 9, 1979, Cardinal Cooke announced that burial would be in the crypt of St. Patrick's, a departure from the one-hundred-year tradition according that honor only to deceased archbishops of New York and rectors of the cathedral.

Just as the work of all of these priests has been central to the ministry of the cathedral, so also has that of the numerous laity who, in various ways, have contributed to the success of that mission. Since April 17, 1817, when the Senate and Assembly of the State of New York granted a charter establishing a corporate entity "in fact and in law by the name... of the Trustees of St. Patrick's Cathedral in the City of New York," the *ex officio* president of that corporation has been the presiding Bishop (Archbishop from 1850 on) of New York.[15] Members of the Board of Trustees, elected for a three-year term, may serve any number of such terms provided there is a recurring sabbatical of one year after each term. By 1979, of the two hundred-and-seventy-nine trustees who had served, most had had more than one term, including some with records of as many as eight, nine or ten terms.[16]

Under the leadership of the reigning ecclesiastic of the Church of New York, the successive members of the Board of Trustees of St. Patrick's Cathedral have concerned themselves with the management of the business affairs of both the old and the new St. Patrick's, as well as with the growing number of cemeteries of the archdiocese. Although the original charter has never been amended, during the 1950's Cardinal Spellman introduced a distinction between what he termed "the church arm" and "the cemetery arm" of the corporation, assigning the latter as the major responsibility of the trustees.[17] Today, with their Executive Director Monsignor Edward J. Mitty and his staff, the trustees continue their valuable service to the archdiocese in the management of its cemeteries as well as in any other capacity in which their talents may be useful to their cardinal archbishop. In 1903, the offices of the Board of Trustees were moved from 266 Mulberry Street, joining the chancery offices and Cathedral College in the renovated building on Madison Avenue between 51st and 52nd Streets, formerly the Boland School.[18] Presently their suite of offices is located on the 17th floor of the new archdiocesan office building on First Avenue beween 55th and 56th Streets.

Since a full chronicling of the efforts of the myriad individuals who have helped to make the history of the cathedral is not possible here, a few examples must suffice to serve as representative of the many. Music, historically an important part of the services at St. Patrick's, has been provided under the direction of five organists, the first of whom, William F. Pecher, came up from the old cathedral. He was succeeded by his assistant, James C. Ungerer who,

when he retired in 1929, had served the cathedral for a total
of thirty-six years and was awarded a pension of $2000 per
annum by the trustees.[19] Pietro Yon, organist and director
of music from 1929 until his death in 1943, was replaced by
Dr. Charles M. Courboin, former head of the Peabody
Conservatory of Music in Baltimore, Maryland, who upon
his retirement in 1970 was succeeded by the present organist
John F. Grady. Traditionally, the cathedral organist and
director of music, with his assistant, have been responsible
for training the choirs that have sung regularly at the High
Mass on Sundays and other special liturgical events.

During the first half of the twentieth century, the 1903
motu proprio of Pius X had prohibited women from being
admitted to such choirs. Thus, much of the liturgical singing
at St. Patrick's had been provided by members of Cathedral
College, St. Patrick's Cathedral Men's Choir and a Boys'
Choir made up of nine-to-seventeen-year olds from the
parish school, and, after the closing of the latter, from St.
Ann's Academy.[20] However, in 1955 and 1958, Pius XII
lifted the earlier restriction and permitted the use of mixed
choirs, or of women's and girls' choirs.[21] Today, about one
hundred men and women volunteers, selected and trained
by John Grady, perform anything from Gregorian chant to
contemporary liturgical music.[22] Recitals and performances
by visiting organists and choirs, presently a part of the
regular calendar of Sunday afternoon events at the cathedral, have featured both American and European, Catholic
and non-Catholic individuals and groups. One of the musical highlights of the centennial celebration at St. Patrick's
was a concert of sacred music by the Concert Society of the
Vienna State Opera Chorus which was attended by more
than 3,000 people.[23]

The perfection of the services at St. Patrick's throughout
its history also owes much to the dedicated work of the
laymen who have served in such capacities as sexton, verger,

sacristan, floral decorator, etc. One of the early sextons, William T. A. Hart, had been connected with the parish from boyhood; before his death in 1897 he conducted a large undertaking establishment at 509 Madison Avenue.[24] Joseph P. Rutledge, who for many years was verger of the cathedral at a salary of $12 a week, at his death in 1905 bequeathed $20,000, the savings of a lifetime, toward the cathedral debt.[25]

Presently, the person on the cathedral staff with the longest tenure is sacristan Bernard Carroll who has served under three of the cathedral's four rectors and three of New York's five cardinals. During the depressed times of the 1930's Bernie found what he then thought would be temporary work at St. Patrick's, but has remained there despite other job opportunities. For more than four decades, Mr. Carroll has prepared the vestments, chalices and other appointments for the priests who celebrate the daily Masses at St. Patrick's. It is a work he says has become "part of my life. When I am not here, I miss the cathedral; I have never minded coming to work."[26] Now in his eighties, Frank Simeola, a Westchesterite who resides in the city of New Rochelle, has been associated with the cathedral since 1949. The artistry of his magnificent floral arrangements for important occasions such as Easter, Christmas, the Feast of St. Patrick, etc. has been widely admired. Although suffering from a severe arthritic condition, Mr. Simeola, known for his friendly smile and gentle sense of humor, still retains his association with the cathedral where he was responsible for the centennial decorations, a feat he considers the culmination of his career.[27]

Perhaps no previous decade in their history had opened more auspiciously for American Catholics than that of the 1960's, marked as it was by the election of John F. Kennedy, the first Catholic to occupy the White House (1961-63) and the pontificate of Pope John XXIII (1958-63) whose call for *aggiornamento* initiated a new era in the history of the Catholic Church At the same time that the youthful Kennedy, without deliberate intent, was instrumental in effecting an end to what was left of the separatist mentality that had characterized the earlier immigrant Church of the United States, the seventy-seven-year-old John XXIII was winning a personal prestige as a kind of father figure for the whole world by his friendly reception of other religious leaders—Protestant, Orthodox and Jewish. His decision to call the ecumenical council, which opened on October 11, 1962, as Vatican Council II, was motivated by a desire to up-date the teaching, discipline and organization of the church in order to bring about the unity of all Christians. By the time the last session of the Council was completed on December 8, 1965, death had claimed both Johns: the Pope on June 3, 1963 from natural causes; the President by an assassin's bullet in Dallas, Texas on November 22, 1963. To their respective successors Paul VI and Lyndon B. Johnson was left the challenge of carrying forward the work they had begun.

Shortly before the close of the Council, the visit of Paul VI to New York (October 4, 1965) was an historic occasion not only for the United Nations where he delivered his "*Jamais plus la guerre!*" message, but also for the people of a country and city never before visited by a pope. During his fourteen hours in the city, which included a motorcade, speeches and religious ceremonies, an estimated four million people gave the pope an enthusiastic welcome. When Paul, with Cardinal Spellman the pope's official host in the Archdiocese of New York, arrived at St. Patrick's for a fifteen-minute welcoming ceremony, the dense crowds in the surrounding streets cheered as the pontiff waved a greeting and blessing from the terrace of the cathedral. Upon entering St. Patrick's, Paul was greeted by an unprecedented burst of applause and cheering from the congrega-

Pope Paul VI at prayer in St. Patrick's, October 4, 1965

tion which included many distinguished members of the hierarchy, clergy and laity. During the busy day that followed, the pope met with President Lyndon Johnson at the Waldorf Astoria Hotel, spent three hours at the United Nations where he delivered a thirty-two minute speech to the members of the General Asembly and their guests and attended a reception during which Mrs. Jacqueline Kennedy was first on the reception line to speak with the pontiff and kiss his ring. After leaving the UN, Paul met with leaders of the Protestant, Jewish and Greek Orthodox faiths in nearby Holy Family Church, offered Mass and preached in Yankee Stadium where some 90,000 people greeted him with thunderous applause, and, enroute to Kennedy Airport, visited the Vatican Pavilion at the World's Fair. At 11:00 P.M., before boarding his plane for the return trip to Rome, Paul expressed his gratitude to all Americans for their "enthusiastic and affectionate welcome;" for their country, he offered "prayerful wishes for prosperity and peace, under the rule of law, in concord with other nations of the world..."[28]

For American Catholics, however, nothing in their past history had prepared them for the revolutionary developments of the post-conciliar period which witnessed the spread of agitation and polarization throughout the American Church over the reforms and innovations introduced by Vatican Council II.[29] Among other divisive issues of these years, the liturgical changes caused widespread discontent among both clergy and laity. Early in 1965, Cardinal Spellman was appealed to as "the spokesman for the Hierarchy of the United States at the Council in Rome" for help in "uniting our Catholic people together as they were before the great changes in our Church."[30] In response to the writer's charges that the "Mass changes [are] separating us, church from church, brother from brother, sister from sister, friend from friend, who were all one before this all started," the cardinal graciously acknowledged the letter, adding "I hope that with the passage of time, the new liturgy will be better understood and people will become more accustomed to its use."[31] Although others sought to interview the cardinal about the Council, he held to the resolution he had made in the very beginning that he "would give no interviews and make no statements, except those actually made during the sessions."[32] Whatever his personal preferences regarding the liturgy, New York's cardinal was among the first bishops of the United States to implement the Council decrees on liturgical reform.[33]

By the centennial year of the cathedral, much of the painful and turbulent mood of the late sixties and early seventies appeared to have subsided. The previous exodus of large numbers of priests and religious from their ministries had dwindled, as had the departure of countless lay Catholics from the Church.[34] Instead, in growing numbers those who considered themselves good Catholics were remaining in the Church, despite a great gap between certain of their own beliefs and practices and the official teaching of the papal and hierarchical magisteriums.[35] These same years brought changes in the leadership of both the archdiocese and the cathedral parish. Following the death of Cardinal Spellman (December 2, 1967), New York's Auxiliary Bishop Terence James Cooke was named Archbishop of New York by Paul VI (March 1968) and, a year later, was made a cardinal, receiving the red hat from Paul VI on April 30, 1969. The latter year also marked the retirement of the cathedral's Bishop Flannelly, who continued to reside in the rectory until his death some four years later. His mortal remains, like those of his predecessor, were interred in the crypt of the cathedral.

Appointed fourth rector of the cathedral in November 1969, Monsignor James F. Rigney, after ordination in 1947, had held a number of teaching assignments before serving, respectively, as secretary to Cardinals Spellman and Cooke (1965-69). Under his leadership, and despite the shortage of priests that characterized the years following Vatican II, the cathedral staff has continued to offer the traditional services for the small number of resident parishioners (about 300) and the many more numerous weekday worshippers, as well as for the steady flow of visitors who tour the cathedral, particularly on Sundays, and other holidays throughout the year. Weekday Masses at St. Patrick's attract more than 1,500 persons each day, while on each Sunday the total Mass attendance averages between five and six thousand people, of whom at least ninety percent are visitors to New York. On one Saturday, a count of the people as they left the cathedral from 7:00 A.M. to 7:00 P.M. reached 27,000, including those who came to attend Mass or simply dropped in for a brief visit, as well as the numerous visitors to New York who made St. Patrick's part of their sight-seeing tour of the city.[36]

In response to the need for more personnel to welcome visitors and provide them with information about St. Patrick's, a special group, known as Cathedral Volunteers, was organized (1974). Members of this group also serve in other capacities such as helping with the publication *Alive and Well...* as well as developing programs for such organizations as St. Patrick's Young at Heart Club for senior citizens. Among other cathedral organizations, the Legion of Mary still meets regularly, as do more recent groups such as Alanon and Debtors Anon, a Charismatic Prayer Group and a Religious Instruction Class.[37] The New Parish House, located at 14 East 51st Street in 1974, provides appropriate meeting places for these groups, while in the cathedral itself the schedule of devotions , other than Masses, includes the Miraculous Medal Novena, Rosary, Scripture Service, and Friday Exposition of the Blessed Sacrament and Benediction at 6:00 P.M., except for First Fridays when Exposition begins after the 7:00 A.M. Mass, with Benediction and Reposition after the 5:30 P.M. Mass.

In addition to the alterations made to accommodate the new liturgical forms introduced after the Council, many other improvements were carried out, enhancing both the interior and exterior of St. Patrick's so that by the centen-

Terence Cardinal Cooke
Archbishop of New York (1968-1983)

nial year Renwick's masterpiece had reached the apogee of its beauty. The 1970's brought a total restoration and renovation of the interior of the cathedral and, with the canonization (1975) of American-born Elizabeth Ann Bayley Seton, foundress of the Sisters of Charity and the first American woman to be so honored, the erection of a shrine in her honor on the 50th Street side of the nave.[38] Four years later, John Neumann, who emigrated from Bohemia to the United States, became an American citizen and served as Bishop of Philadelphia (1852-60), was canonized and his shrine was located on the 51st Street side of the cathedral. For the popular St. Anthony of Padua, a new bronze statue was designed and executed, replacing the older one which over the years continued to attract more devotees than any other shrine in the cathedral. Meanwhile, the finishing touches had been put to the Lady Chapel with the completion of a beautifully executed statue of the Virgin Mary which was put in place on its roof. Such was the perfection of the cathedral as it entered its second century of service that the Municipal Art Society of New York presented its 1981 award to St. Patrick's with the following citation:

> Never in the lifetime of anyone now walking the streets of this city has St. Patrick's Cathedral looked so beautiful. It is immaculate within and without, and the copper figure of the Virgin Mary...above the roof of the Lady Chapel, is a sign of the affection in which the Cathedral is held by its priestly guardians. She smiles down upon us as we hurry past along Madison Avenue; her smile is a benediction, for in her presence everything we look upon is blest.[39]

That Archbishop Hughes' dream of "a cathedral in the city of New York that may be worthy of our increasing numbers, intelligence, and wealth as a religious community,

Photograph by James Heffernan

Governor Hugh Carey, Cardinal Cooke, Monsignor James Rigney,
Mayor Edward Koch and Walter Cronkite at the opening of
the centenary celebrations in 1978

and...as a public architectural monument of the present and prospective greatness of this metropolis" had been fully realized became abundantly clear as St. Patrick's began its year-long celebration of one hundred years of service in New York. On November 1, 1978, at noon on the steps of the cathedral Mayor Edward Koch, on behalf of the citizens of New York City, inaugurated a city-wide celebration, proclaiming the twelve months ahead to be "St. Patrick's Cathedral One Hundredth Year Celebration." Referring to the cathedral as "an enduring symbol of spiritual strength," Koch declared "we New Yorkers...of all religions and every nationality...live, work and worship according to our customs...in friendship and freedom...and St. Patrick's has led the way to create that kind of climate."[40] A new "Cornerstone of the Future"[41] was dedicated by Cardinal Cooke, while standing by were Monsignor Rigney,

Mayor Koch, Governor Hugh Carey, Walter Cronkite and Alton Marshall, president of Rockefeller Center. On behalf of the Fifth Avenue Association and the Committee of Neighbors, Marshall spoke of the cathedral as "a cornerstone for Fifth Avenue, this neighborhood, Rockefeller Center and for all of New York City," adding "St. Patrick's to us is more than a building. It is an important New York City institution, a popular tourist attraction, an oasis of quiet and inspiration; it is a place of hopes, dreams and aspirations."[42]

During the year-long observance of the centennial, each month featured a special kind of celebration, attracting large numbers to the cathedral and including many representatives of the parishes and schools of the archdiocese. At the major liturgical celebration on May 12 which lasted two hours, the more than 3,000 persons in attendance heard prayers in Gaelic, German, Polish, Chinese, English, Italian and Spanish from the High Altar, while the musical selections ranged from the Gregorian chant of the Creed to a Spanish hymn accompanied by tambourine and guitar, and an ancient Irish melody, the words of which have been attributed to St. Patrick. Both in Cardinal Cooke's homily and the remarks of the Apostolic Delegate to the United States, Archbishop Jean Jadot, emphasis was placed on the role of the cathedral in the life of the city and its millions of immigrants.

Archbishop Jadot, recalling how he, too, had "experienced the extended, warm welcome of the Cathedral," stressed its role in providing "the poor and the destitute, the rich and the mighty, men and women of every race and kind with the gifts of reconciliation and peace." The Gospel of the Mass was read by Roosevelt Spann, the first Black New Yorker to be ordained as a permanent deacon. Also present for the celebration were distinguished representatives of other faiths, tangible evidence of some of the progress made in ecumenism in the post-conciliar years. These included

Bishop Philotheas of the Greek Orthodox Church of North and South America; the Right Reverend Stuart Wetmore, Episcopal Suffragan of New York; Metropolitan Theodosius of the Russian Orthodox Church in America; Archbishop Torkom Manoogian, Primate, Diocese of the Armenian Church; and The Reverend James A. Graefe, Metropolitan New York Synod, Lutheran Church in America.[43] Four months later, Monsignor Rigney announced that St. Patrick's would host an inter-faith service as part of the welcome of the religious community of New York to the Dalai Lama. Pointing out that while the cathedral had witnessed many ecumenical events, the greeting to the Dalai Lama would be the "first inter-faith service directly involving the Buddhist community" and, according to the rector, would "in its own way [be] responsive to Pope John Paul II who... made clear his wish for ever-deepening ecumenical and inter-faith commitments."[44]

The following October, as the close of the year-long celebration drew near, the historic two-day visit of Pope John Paul II to New York added a unique dimension of hope and joy to the centennial observance for all New Yorkers. At the request of Cardinal Cooke, Father Edwin O'Brien of the Cathedral Rectory coordinated the New York program of activities for the Holy Father's visit. The schedule as finally worked out provided for "a pastoral visit, with opportunities both to see and be seen by a maximum of people, and to gather in prayer with the flock he tends" that had been expressly requested by Rome. In addition, it aimed "to offer his Holiness a glimpse and even an experience of what it means to be a Catholic in New York..."[45] The pleasure with which John Paul II looked forward to his visit to the United States, expressed in a message to President Jimmy Carter as the papal plane entered the air space over the United States, was matched many times more for New Yorkers during his stay in their city.

As it turned out, the only thing lacking for the New York

papal visit was good weather, but despite the bleak, rainy and windswept conditions the scheduled events took place and the crowds were there to see and judge for themselves. Countless attempts were made, before and after the papal visit, to analyze its meaning and effect upon the city and its people. Some Protestant and Jewish leaders had early raised the question of how John Paul II's religious zeal would be received by non-Catholics in our highly pluralistic country. Subsequent to his visit in New York City and elsewhere, that question was answered by a wave of praise from many of these same leaders. Among them, the Reverend William Sloane Coffin, Pastor of the Riverside Church in Manhattan, noted "an ecumenical spirit" in the Pope and "a very deep humanity that speaks to the longing for genuine charity and wisdom." The President of the Lutheran Church in America, Dr. James Crumley, believed that "the Pope was meeting the real issues head on—housing, the poor, unemployment." Rabbi Wolfe Kelman, leader of the conservative Rabinnical Assembly, while not sure that John Paul II was the innovator the Church had in John XXIII, added "All I know is that my son Levi, a young rabbi who is going to Israel, attended the service in St. Patrick's Cathedral and said that he got tremendous spiritual vibrations from the Pope. I feel the same way. He has a tremendous love for people."[46] No doubt millions of other Americans, of all creeds, across the country would say "Amen" to that!

Although one of the main thrusts of Vatican II was ecumenism, progress in achieving Christian unity has been slow in the area of settling the differences that exist in theological dialogue. Meanwhile, however, many gains have been made in the relationships between Christian churches in the New York area, as elsewhere. When, during the centennial year, Monsignor Rigney compared ecumenism in 1879 with that of 1979, he noted that the former year was "quite without ecumenical or inter-faith interest." In

1979, however, things were quite different for "not only Christians but people of all religious traditions actively seek deeper mutual understanding and opportunities to be together in prayer and work." Accordingly, he proposed that as a goal for the new decade "St. Patrick's should not only participate but hopefully lead in responding to the impulse of the Spirit."[47]

About six months later, the International Roman Catholic-Lutheran Commission's statement that "Catholics and Lutherans have discovered that they have a common mind on basic doctrinal truths, which points to Jesus Christ, the living center of our faith" was received with rejoicing in New York. In June 1982, in St. Patrick's Cathedral, Lutherans and Roman Catholics met for a joint observance of the faith they share and to express their joy in the present and hopes for the future.[48] A few months later, Brother Roger, founder of the ecumenical monastic community of Taize, France, was welcomed to the cathedral by the religious community of New York for a special gathering marking the beginning of the United States phase of Brother Roger's Pilgrimage of Reconciliation.[49] More recently, a series of "neighborly dialogues" was inaugurated and the results shared with readers of *Alive and Well*. Among those interviewed was the Rector of St. Thomas Episcopal Church, Father John Andrew, who expressed the hope that St. Patrick's and St. Thomas's might become closer, adding "I long for the day when Anglican orders will be recognized as valid. . . then I can come and concelebrate with the people I love."[50] When Dr. Bryant M. Kirkland, Senior Minister of Fifth Avenue Presbyterian Church, was asked what he thought St. Patrick's might do to meet the needs of the neighborhood, he replied "I would like the Cathedral to continue to offer ecumenical hospitality as it has in the past because this provides for an expression of fraternity."[51]

In his homily at Yankee Stadium on October 2nd, Pope

John Paul II had emphasized that "social thinking and social practice inspired by the Gospel" must always be marked by a "special sensitivity towards those who are most in distress...extremely poor...suffering from all the physical, mental and moral ills that afflict humanity, including hunger, neglect, unemployment and despair." He went on to remind his listeners that "there are many [such] in your own midst" and insisted that the form of charitable aid must retain "its irreplaceable character as a fraternal and personal encounter with those who are in distress [as well as] respectful of the freedom and dignity of those being helped."[52] In the fall of 1979, Monsignor Rigney and his Cathedral Volunteers set about to inaugurate a program which they called "Our Neighbors." That same October, Eleanor Connolly of the New York City Department for the Aging arrived at St. Patrick's to help establish an information and referral service for older people in conjunction with St. Patrick's "Our Neighbor's" program. Within a year, this so-called Midtown Information for Senior Citizens (MISC) had helped more than one thousand older adults, as well as assisting with the social service work for "Our Neighbors."[53]

The problems of these people are neither new nor easily solved. During the sixties and seventies, as the needy and welfare population of the city increased dramatically, many older adults were moved to what had formerly served as hotels and brownstone residences in midtown, following the takeover and conversion of them into Single Room Occupancy (SRO's) housing by the city. In a recent study entitled *Outposts of the Forgotten*, the appalling conditions in these SRO's and the devastating effects upon those who live in them are described in detail.[54] As the cathedral enters its second century of service, it has established as one of its firm goals "No one forgotten or abandoned in our neighborhood."[55] A good start has been made with a recent survey of the parish which confirmed the fact that "a great number of aging people are living alone. A great many never venture more than one block from where they live. Above all, they are afraid; afraid initially even to respond to someone offering friendship." However, Monsignor Rigney has expressed confidence that the "people of St. Patrick's Cathedral parish will see to the rightful and Christian care of these aging people."[56] At the moment it may not be clear what kind of action will help these people, but what the cathedral staff sees very clearly is that these people will not be helped by silence and inaction.

More than one hundred years of skill and care have been put into the building of St. Patrick's, making the Cathedral Church of New York one that neither believer nor unbeliever may pass through untouched. People of all kinds have found a sense of eternity as they enter its portals and find solace where so many others had come before seeking easement in distress. Countless others come to express gratitude for some good fortune, such as the young construction worker who was rescued from almost certain death recently when fire trapped him on the top floors of Trump Towers, a building under construction on Fifth Avenue and 57th Street. Interviewed by a reporter later and asked how he planned to celebrate, he responded without a moment's hesitation: "I think I'll stop off at St. Pat's and say a little prayer."[57] Down the long corridor of its history, as successive archbishops, rectors, priests, trustees and lay men and women have been associated with its mission as workers or friends, the cathedral has indeed been maintained as one of the most beautiful spired structures in our land, while at the same time it has become something that is personal and real to those who visit and pray within its walls.

APPENDIX I

*Trustees are elected for a three-year term; a sabbatical of one year is
required between each successive term.

147

William Lummis — 1895-97; 1904-10*

John G. Agar — 1896-98; 1901-19*

Dr. E. L. Keyes — 1896-98

Frederick R. Coudert — 1896-98

John A. Sullivan — 1898-1900

Hon. John Hayes — 1898-1900

Cornelius O'Reilly — 1898-1900

Thomas L. Feitner — 1899; 1901-1927*

Thomas J. Keveney — 1899

John A. McCreery, M.D. — 1900-02

James Devlin — 1900-02; 1906-08

James Ross Curran — 1900-01

Stephen J. Geoghegan — 1901-03

John F. O'Rourke — 1901-15*; 1919-33*

Hugh Grant — 1902-04

John Fox — 1903-13*

James A. Farley — 1904-10*; 1915-21*; 1923

William F. Sheehan — 1904

Thomas F. Ryan — 1905-07

Louis H. Amy — 1906-16*; 1918-19

James Devlin — 1906-08

George J. Gillespie, Sr. — 1911-13; 1916-50*

Alfonse de Navarro — 1912-14; 1917-23*

Ernest Iselin — 1912-18*; 1935-49*

Bernard F. Coleman — 1915-17

Thomas F. Farrell — 1919-43*

Cornelius Tiers — 1919-1920

John C. Neeser — 1920-34*

George H. Fearons — 1921-30*

William J. Bowe — 1922-40*

Cornelius F. Kelly — 1922-56*

Thomas A. Reynolds — 1922-32*; 1934

George MacDonald — 1924-61*

Victor J. Dowling — 1924-34*

Charles M. Early — 1925-51*

Gerald M. Borden — 1931; 1933-47*

Bruno Benziger — 1933-51*

John Moody — 1934; 1936-50*

Frank P. Walsh — 1935-39*

Carl Ahlstrom — 1936-38

Dr. Raymond P. Sullivan — 1939-40; 1942-63*

Hugh Grant — 1940-41; 1946-56*

John J. Reynolds — 1942-44; 1958-80*

Joseph B. Lynch — 1942; 1944-54*; 1956

George J. Gillespie, Jr. — 1944-65*

Thomas J. Ross — 1949-75*

John Madden — 1951; 1953-79*

Harry C. Hagerty — 1951-77*

Hon. William T. Collins — 1952-58*

Robert J. Marony — 1952-58*

Hon. John E. McGeehan — 1953-55; 1958-68*

Paolino Gerli — 1957-79*

John A. Coleman — 1957-77*

James A. Farley — 1960-74*

Joseph F. Higgins — 1960-61

J. Paul Carey — 1962; 1964-73*

George H. Fearons — 1963-73*

Dr. Maurice J. Costello — 1963

Joseph Martino 1964; 1966-68; 1970

Victor D. Ziminsky — 1968-81*

John F. Connolly — 1970-72

Thomas A. Coleman — 1974; 1975-81*

Eugene J. Leone — 1974-80*

Richard R. Shinn — 1974-80*

William M. Ellinghaus — 1977-79

Hon. Harold A. Stevens — 1977-78

Malcolm Wilson — 1978

T. Vincent Learson — 1978

John M. Joyce — 1979-81

APPENDIX II

The Cathedral Priests

1879-1979

Patrick V. Ahern 1954
Francis J. Ansbro 1959-61

John J. Barry 1961-66; 1972-73
Myles Burke 1946
Francis Breidenbach 1966-69
Edwin B. Broderick 1947-57
John J. Byrne 1906-16

Richard A. Cahill (Chapel)
1969-72; 1976-79
Michael R. Carleo 1968
Thomas G. Carroll 1912-17
Martin de Porres Clark, O.F.M.,
Cap. 1975
James V. Cleary, O.M.I., 1973
Christian Cochini, S.J., 1977
James N. Connolly 1889-96
Edward M. Connors 1951
Bernard Corcoran 1918
Michael E. Crimmins 1975-76
Francis X. Cronin 1958-67
John K. Crotty 1952-53

Patrick Daly 1889-98; 1914-21
William J. B. Daly 1886-1902
Edward V. Dargin 1924-27
Michael J. Deacy 1939-54

Bernard P. Donachie 1955-66
Thomas A. Donnellan 1942-56
John G. Donohue (Chapel)
1960-66
Cornelius T. Donovan 1879-84
William L. Doty 1955-57
Francis X. Duffy 1950-69
Thomas J. Dunphy 1885
D. Marcus Dyer 1898-1902

Francis A. Fadden 1919-30
John E. Fanning (Chapel) 1979
Gerard Ferrante 1891-1920
Joseph F. Flannelly 1938
John M. Fleming 1948
Timothy J. Flynn 1948-50
Vincent J. Fox 1959-70
Philip J. Furlong 1946

Michael F. Gallagher 1970-74
Charles A. Genet 1971-72
Charles E. Giblin 1946
Robert Gilhooly 1967
Thomas L. Graham 1928-43
William T. Greene 1944-55
James P. Griffin 1952
James H. Griffiths 1943-48
George Guilfoyle 1944

Leo F. Halpin (Chapel) 1978
Henry F. Hammer 1917-37
Edward P. Hauck 1955
Patrick J. Hayes 1906-13
Richard O. Hughes 1903-10
William F. Hughes 1910-14

Walter P. Kellenberg 1934-46
John A. Kellner 1887-92
James W. Kelly 1880-90
John Kelly (Chapel) 1966-68
Neal Kerrigan, O.F.M. Cap.,
   1976-78
William F. King 1940-42

Anthony Lammel 1879-86
Michael J. Lavelle 1879-86
James V. Lewis 1907-12
Oscar V. Lynch 1957-59

Patrick P. McAleer 1901-02
Charles J. McCabe 1926-28
Thomas J. McCloskey 1887-88
Edward J. McCorry 1962-66
Charles G. McDonagh 1967-69
Charles E. McDonnell 1879-86
Bryan J. McEntegart 1923-25;
   1941-42
Vincent de Paul McGean 1915-16
Thomas J. McGovern 1962-70
Daniel J. McMackin 1903-08
Bernard J. McMahon 1956
Joseph H. McMahon 1886-1900
Thomas J. McMahon 1943-45
Charles J. McManus 1947-61
John A. McManus 1962-65
Dennis McNelis, C.S.C., 1969-70
Bernard F. McQuade 1907-27

James McQuirk 1879
Thomas F. Maher 1944-47
Charles J. Mahoney, C.S.C.,
   1973-
James P. Mahoney 1971-73
Bernard M. Martin 1947-48
William B. Martin 1907-22
John S. Middleton 1947-51
Thomas A. Modugno 1977-
Robert Moher 1966-74
M. J. Mulhern 1884-88
Francis J. Murphy 1946-49
Thomas F. Murphy 1890-1906
John J. Murray (Chapel) 1967-
   72
Thomas F. Myhan 1897-1901

John J. Nestor 1933
Henry T. Newry 1894-1900
Thomas A. Nielson 1974-

Edwin F. O'Brien 1976-
Joseph P. O'Brien 1962-70
William B. O'Brien (Chapel)
   1956-60
Gregory O'Connor (Chapel)
   1969-72
John O'Hare, O.F.M. Cap.,
   1979-

Donald J. Poulin 1971
Raymond T. Powers 1957-58

John M. J. Quinn 1915-30

Robert J. Redmond (Chapel)
   1976-
Francis F. Reh 1939-40

Joseph H. Rostagno 1929-33

Gustav Schultheiss 1948
William A. Scully 1940-44
William J. Sinnott 1903-14
Francis X. Shea 1940-42
Michael J. Shea 1913-14
E. S. Slattery 1884-86
Walter D. Slattery 1917

Charles O'Connor Sloane 1937-38

James Thornton, S. J., 1976-77
Joseph A. Tytheridge 1929-39

Edward J. Waterson 1952-53
Christopher J. Weldon 1945-48
Harry J. Wolff 1950-65
Robert E. Woods 1922-46

APPENDIX III

Bro. Donatif Flavian Abgrall
(1914-18)

Bro. Augustine Ralph Ballentine
(1914-15)

Bro. Bernadine of Jesus Banfield
1913-14)

Bro. Binen Alphonsus Barrete
(1882-84)

Bro. Augustine George Bennett
(1920-23)

Bro. Claudius James Bernache
(1936-37;40-41)

Bro. Arthur Berchmans Biller
(1932-33;40)

Bro. Anselm of Jesus Bisson
(1915-18)

Bro. Daniel of Jesus Boegolea
(1898-99)

Bro. Divitien Bourel
(1911-13)

Bro. Albert William Boyle
(1882-92)

Bro. Angelus Raphael Brady
(1905-07)

Bro. Albinus of Mary Brartou
(1892-93)

Bro. Alexander Joseph Brennan
(1934-37)

Bro. Bernadine of Mary Brennan
(1897-98)

Bro. Adelphus Michael Brewin
(1926)

Bro. Clement Benignus Brown
(1914)

Bro. Bernard Juilian Brunelle
(1938-45)

Bro. Bonaventure Anthony
Buckley, (1925-27)

Bro. Bertram Herbert Byrne
(1899-1900)

Bro. Benjamin Joseph Carey
(1916-17)

Bro. Ambrose of Mary Carroll
(1927-28)

Bro. Adolphus of Mary Casey
(1882-85)

Bro. Angelus Gabriel Cashin
(1914-16)

Bro. Albert Andrew Cassidy
(1891-92)

Bro. Auxilius William
Cavanaugh (1934)

Bro. Amedy Bernard Collins
(1908)

Bro. Amedy Bernard Conway
(1925)

Bro. Alfred of Jesus Cragin
(1934-35)
Bro. Clementian Felix Curran
(1902)

Bro. Abracian Denis Daley
(1910-13)
Bro. Alician Joseph Daly
(1882-84)
Bro. Aquilimus Joseph Danaher
(1931-37)
Bro. Barbas Patrick Driscoll
(1913-16)
Bro. Cesarius Michael Duffy
(1911-14)
Bro. Bonitus Duggan
(1916-19)

Bro. Euthymius Alban English
(1882-84)

Bro. Bardomian John Fahey
(1883; 1924-25)
Bro. Basilidas Joseph
Featherstone (1901-02)
Bro. Austin William Flanagan
(1921-22)
Bro. Cleophas Luke Flanagan
(1903)
Bro. Cronus James Flynn
(1902)

Bro. Benignus of Jesus Gerrity
(1930-?)
Bro. Andrew Philip Girard
(Principal, 1930-36)
Bro., Arthur Philip Grimley
(1914-15)

Bro. Arcadius Walter Guthrie
(1913-14)
Bro. Alphonsus Edwin Haugh
(1914-20)
Bro. Alphonsus Roch Hayes
(1901)
Bro. Augustus Victor Healy
(1889-95)
Bro. Columban of Mary Hession
(1923-27)
Bro. Albert Gerard Horn
(1934-38)
Bro. Charisius Norbert
Humphries (1927-29)
Bro. Abracian Hunt (1884-85)

Bro. Decorose Henri Jacob
(1906-07)
Bro. Conrad Henry Johnston
(1929-?)
Bro. Dalmace Marie Jolliet
(1913;1921-22)

Bro. Conrad Gabriel Kane
(1933)
Bro. Basil Polycarp Kane
(1900)
Bro. Andrew Stephen Kapp
(1935-37)
Bro. Amandus Henry Kargl
(1922-27; Principal, 1927-29)
Bro. Ambrose Kealty
(1887-88)
Bro. Christopher Charles Kearns
(1901-03)
Bro. Augustus Leo Kelly
(1909-13)

Bro. Albert Matthew Kerins
(1934-39)
Bro. Galdinian Walter Kueuy
(1899)

Bro. Basil Leo Lee
(1937-39)
Bro. Binen Michael Lenihan
(Principal, 1916-19)
Bro. Bernard William Leonard
(1939-40)
Bro. Oliver Xavier Luiset
(1915-21)

Bro. Celian Anselm McArthur
(1895-97)
Bro. Alfred Patrick McAuliffe
(1923-24)
Bro. Clarence Vincent
McConville (1939-41)
Bro. Augustine Paul McDermott
(1937)
Bro. Basil Stephen McDonald
(1904)
Bro. Benignus Austin McGeehan
(Principal, 1889-98)
Bro. Azades Raphael McGinn
(1939-41)
Bro. Bonaventure McGinty
Thomas (1917-19)
Bro. Cyprian Andrew McManus
(1935-36)
Bro. Azer Cyril Maher
(1893)
Bro. Cecilian Patrick Martin
(1937-40)
Bro. Bernadine Francis Mead
(1915-20)

Bro. Cletus Joseph Meyer
(1922-24)
Bro. Abracian Denis Mulligan
(1929-?)
Bro. Alban Anthony Mulvihill
(1902)
Bro. Donatian Joseph Murphy
(1914-15)
Bro. Isaac John Murphy
(Principal, 1882-89)

Bro. Adelbert Francis Needham
(1912-13; 1929)
Bro. Albeus Jerome Needham
(1889)
Bro. Adelbert Patrick Neville
(1897-1903; Principal, 1912-15;
1919-22)

Bro. Eumenius Leo O'Regan
(1904-05)

Bro. Benedict Hugh Petrie
(1896-98)
Bro. Anthimus Gregory Phelan
(1884-87)
Bro. Augustine William Prange
(1935-39)
Bro. Cornelius Luke Pryor
(Principal, 1922-27)

Bro. Corbinian Joseph Quinn
(1906-18)

Bro. Clarence of Mary Rafferty
(1915-16)
Bro. Basileus Francis Reilly
(1889-91)

Bro. Blaise Austin Roach (1884–
98; Principal, 1898-1902;
1915-16)

Bro. Bernard of Mary Ryan
(Principal, 1936-38)

Bro. Arnold Edward Saunders
(Principal, 1902-04)

Bro. Bernard Eugene Schultz
(1899-1900)

Bro. Alban Faber Shallew
(Principal, 1904-12)

Bro. Arthur Philip Smith
(1933)

Bro. Anthony of Mary Sullivan
(1908-10)

Bro. Albert George Sweeney,
(Principal, 1929-30)

Bro. Adelphus Joseph Veno
(Principal, 1938-41)

Bro. Alphonsus of Mary
Wachalski (1933-?)

Bro. Albinus Peter Walsh
(1882-86)

Bro. Basilian of Mary Wehage
(1889)

Bro. Finan Whelan
(1909-11; 1930-?)

Bro. Aubert of Jesus Zehetner
(1927-28)

APPENDIX IV

Sisters of Charity Who Taught at Cathedral School

1882-1940

Sr. Mary Estelle Ballance
(1929-31)
Sr. Mary Clement Barry
(1932-38)
Sr. Regina Rose Brull (1906-10)

Sr. Mary Paul Cantwell
(1900-22)
Sr. Mary Beata Cassidy
(1908-18)
Sr. Agnes Marita Costello
(1929-30)
Sr. Marita Agnes Crew
(1931-40)
Sr. Mary Myra Cross
(1934-36)
Sr. Loretto Anna Cunningham
(1898-1904; 1919-31)

Sr. Louise Carmela Daly
(1912-13)
Sr. Mary Mercedes Donovan
(1921-29)
Sr. Mary Isabel Dowdell
(1937-39)

Sr. Margaret Viola Foley
(1900-12)

Sr. Mary Pauline Garrety
(1882-95)
Sr. Rose Mercedes Gillespie
(1906-14)

Sr. Mary Raymond Hennessy
(1882-85; Principal, 1885-1919)
Sr. Mary Benedict Hickey
(1913-15)
Sr. Mary Martha Hickey
(Principal, 1882-85)
Sr. Cecilia Borgia Horan
(1929-32)

Sr. Mary Alphonsette Keefe
(1932-34)
Sr. Mary Liguori Kennedy
(1910-15)
Sr. Mary Victoire Kerby
(Principal, 1919-27)
Sr. Marie Joseph Kilpatrick
(1882-94)
Sr. Constance Marie Kirby
(1903)

Sr. Marie Consolata Leifels
(1913-21)
Sr. Angela Mary Lyons
(1922-29)

Sr. Stella Vincent McAlpin (1916-18)

Sr. Mary Celestine McCall (1918-38)

Sr. Marita Aloysia McCann (1927-29)

Sr. Miriam Josita McKenna (1907-23)

Sr. Dolores Magdalen McLoughlin (1901-23)

Sr. Ambrose Rosaire McQuade (1913-27)

Sr. Mary Winifred Maguire (1918)

Sr. Agnes Bernardine Murphy (1929-39)

Sr. Mary Giovanni Murphy (1901-02;08-22)

Sr. Noella Rosaire O'Connor (1910-11)

Sr. Matthew Mary Reynolds (1895-1907)

Sr. Marie Annette Scanlon (1904-06)

Sr. Maria John Sullivan (1936-40)

Sr. Mary Evangeline Tiernan (1923-31)

Sr. Mary Borromeo Tierney (1895-1900)

Sr. Assumpta Maria Tobin (1906-27; Principal, 1927-40)

Sr. Mary Paul Tynan (1910-11)

Sr. Joseph Maria Walls (1930-37)

Sr. Maria Bernard Weir (1882-94)

Sr. Mary Mecrina Willett (1933-36)

NOTES AND REFERENCES

Chapter I (pp. 1-24)

[1] AANY, Henry J. Browne's typescript of uncompleted biography of Archbishop John Hughes, Chapter IV, 14.

[2] On April 8, 1808, Pope Pius VII signed the bulls dividing the See of Baltimore and erecting the new Sees of New York, Philadelphia, Boston and Bardstown.

[3] The definitive biography of Hughes has yet to be written. Browne's nine chapters are the best source for the period covered. *Cf.* John R. G. Hassard, *Life of the Most Reverend John Hughes* (New York, 1866); Henry A. Brann, *Most Reverend John Hughes* (New York, 1892); and Richard Shaw, *Dagger John* (New York, 1977).

[4] According to a Joseph Idley, later sexton of St. Peter's Church, his house on Wall street was used by Father Farmer for the celebration of Mass. *Cf.* William Harper Bennett, *Catholic Footsteps in Old New York: A Chronicle of Catholicity in the City of New York from 1524-1808* (New York, 1909), 338. There is, however, little evidence to support the belief that Farmer entered New York before the Revolution. *Cf.* John F. Quirk, "Father Ferdinand Farmer," United States Catholic Historical Society, *Historical Records and Studies*, VI, Pt. II, 238. Hereafter, this work will be cited as *Records and Studies*.

[5] John M. Farley, *History of St. Patrick's Cathedral* (New York, 1922), 4. Hereafter this work will be cited as *St. Patrick's*.

[6] Whelan received temporary faculties from Carroll on April 16, 1785. These were confirmed by a letter from Rome, dated June 4, 1785; thereafter Carroll was empowered to use his own discretion in such matters. Peter Guilday, *The Life and Times of John Carroll* (New York, 1922), I, 255; also, James Roosevelt Bayley, *A Brief Sketch of the Early History of the Catholic Church on the Island of New York*, 2nd Ed. (New York, 1973), 59.

[7] Guilday, *Carroll*, I, 267.

[8] Farley, *St. Patrick's*, 12.

[9] Leo F. Ryan, *Old St. Peter's* (New York, 1935), 53-55.

[10] Thomas F. Meehan, "Tales of Old New York," *Records and Studies*, XVIII, 1928, 121ff.

[11]Under a revision of state laws in 1801, a test law required all civil and military officers of New York to renounce and abjure allegiance and subjection "in all matters ecclesiastical and civil, to any person or State." When Francis Cooper refused to take such an oath, the Catholics of the city, at a meeting on January 6, 1805, drew up a petition asking the State Assembly and Senate to remove this legal restriction against a religious group. Despite opposition from the Federalist Party in the Legislature, the bill passed the Assembly on February 4 by a large majority and received only one dissenting vote in the Senate.

[12]After the acquisition of Louisiana in 1803, Carroll, for the second time, recommended the creation of new sees, suggesting to Rome nominees for three of the four sees (Boston, Philadelphia and Bardstown), but refraining from naming anyone for New York because "among the priests there, he saw none fit to be entrusted with the episcopate." Guilday, *Carroll*, II, 630.

[13]AAB, 2-T-1. A note on this letter, in the handwriting of Carroll, states that it was received on October 11, 1808. Victor F. O'Daniel, O.P., "Concanen's Election to the See of New York," *Catholic Historical Review*, I (April, 1915), 36, note 27. Hereafter cited as *CHR*.

[14]J. Wilfred Parsons, S.J., "Father Anthony Kohlmann, S.J.," *CHR*, IV (April, 1919), 41.

[15]This title was adopted by the congregation on April 23, 1789, after it was decided that the original one, "The Trustees of the Roman Catholic Church in the City of New York," was too vague.

[16]Thomas A. Janvier, *In Old New York* (New York, 1894), 67-68.

[17]O'Daniel, *loc. cit.*, 43.

[18]Kohlmann to Carroll, October 12, 1810. *Records* of American Catholic Historical Society, XX (1909), 282.

[19]As in the choice of Concanen, Rome had again made no effort to ascertain the wishes of Carroll and his suffragans before appointing Connolly. Moreover, Connolly, a British subject, was appointed when England and the United States were at war.

[20]Connolly's arrival in New York after the signing of the Treaty of Ghent (December, 1814) led some to believe that it was his fear of being treated as an alien enemy that led him to delay so long. John Gilmary Shea, *History of the Catholic Church in the United States* (New York, 1892), III, 176.

[21] *United States Catholic Historical Magazine*, IV (1892), 187. Hereafter cited as *Catholic Historical Magazine*.

[22] *United States Catholic Miscellany*, III (December, 1824), 48.

[23] Farley, *St. Patrick's*, 72.

[24] Ryan, *op. cit.*, 237-38.

[25] In January, 1826, the Free School Society officially changed its name to "The Public School Society," but kept its status as a private corporation.

[26] Ryan, *op.cit.*, 246.

[27] "Minutes of the Trustees of St. Patrick's Cathedral in the City of New York," Office of the Trustees of St. Patrick's Cathedral, New York, 17 vols., 1817-1976, vol. 2, April 4, 1849. Hereafter cited as "Trustees Minutes."

[28] Charles I. White, *Life of Mrs. Eliza A. Seton* (Baltimore, 1879), 372; 480, n. 24.

[29] Trustees Minutes, vol. 1, March 18, 1820.

[30] Connolly to Leonard Neale, New York, February 13, 1817, *Catholic Historical Magazine* IV (1892), 192-93.

[31] *Cf.* Patrick J. Dignan, *History of the Legal Incorporation of Catholic Church Property in the United States, 1784-1932* (New York, 1935), 64.

[32] *An Act to Incorporate the Members of the Religious Society of Roman Catholics Belonging to the Congregation of St. Patrick's Cathedral in the City of New York* (New York, 1817). Under the charter of incorporation Thomas Stoughton, Andrew Morris, Benjamin Disaubry, Michael Bannon, David Atkinson, James R. Mullany, Thomas Glover, Anthony Duff and Joseph Idley were elected to the first board.

[33] Connolly to Archbishop Ambrose Maréchal, New York, 1819, *Catholic Historical Magazine*, IV (1892), 195-98; Peter Guilday, "Trusteeism," *Records and Studies*, XVIII (1928), 7-73.

[34] Guilday, *loc.cit.*, 71.

[35] Cardinal de Somaglia to Maréchal, May 7, 1825, Archives of Georgetown University, 31.9, cited in Ryan, *op.cit.*, 154.

³⁶It was not unusual at this time for two or more priests to exercise the duties of rector in common. However, a decree of the first Provincial Council of Baltimore, held in 1829, outlawed this practice. *Concilia Provincialia Baltimori habita ab anno 1829 usque ad annum 1849* (Baltimore, 1851), 74.

³⁷*Catholic Historical Magazine*, I (1889), 301.

³⁸Meehan, "Catholic Literary New York," *CHR*, IV (January, 1919), 410.

³⁹Peter Guilday, *The Life and Times of John England* (New York, 1924), I, 444. Hereafter cited as *England.*

⁴⁰Charles G. Herbermann, "The Right Reverend John Dubois," *Records and Studies*, I (1899), 278ff.

⁴¹Guilday, *England*, I, 445-46.

⁴²Herbermann, "Dubois," *loc.cit.*, 310.

⁴³*Truth Teller*, July 18, 25, August 1, 1829.

⁴⁴The deed for the church property was conveyed to the bishop, an act which further prejudiced the trustees against him. Dubois to Lyons Association for the Propagation of the Faith, *Records and Studies*, V (1907), 218.

⁴⁵The sum obtained from Propaganda was used to pay for the site of the seminary at Nyack; between 1830-40, the French Society for the Propagation of the Faith contributed approximately $30,000, while the Ludwig-Missionsverein, whose contributions were given mostly to religious orders, also contributed more than 4400 guldens to the churches of the secular clergy. *Cf.* John Edward Hickey, *The Society for the Propagation of the Faith* (Washington, D.C., 1922), 153; and Theodore Roemer, *The Ludwig-Missionsverein and the Church in the United States* (Washington, D.C., 1933), 104.

⁴⁶New York *Observer*, August 17, 1833.

⁴⁷Ray Allen Billington, "Maria Monk and Her Influence," *CHR*, XXII (October, 1936), 283.

⁴⁸Ryan, *op.cit.*, 172.

[49]John Talbot Smith, *The Catholic Church in New York* (New York, 1905), I, 132.

[50]Trustees Minutes, vol. 2, February 5, 1834. John Shea was the father of the historian of the American Church, John Gilmary Shea, who later wrote of his father: "I hope I have repaired any scandal he gave..." *Cf.* Guilday, "John Gilmary Shea," *Records and Studies*, XVII (1926), 12.

[51]Trustees Minutes, vol. 2, October 23, 1834.

[52]*Ibid.*, November 9, December 3, 1834; March 4, 1835; October 8, 1837; March 5, 1839; June 24, 1840.

[53]Herbermann, "Dubois," *loc.cit.*, 278-335.

[54]New York *Mirror*, July 13, 1839; Susan E. Lyman, *The Story of New York* (New York, 1964), 274.

[55]In 1847, the first division of the diocese cut off the northern and western portions of the state, creating the Dioceses of Albany and Buffalo; in 1853, the erection of the Sees of Brooklyn and Newark removed Long Island and Newark.

[56]Henry J. Browne (Ed,), "The Archdiocese of New York a Century Ago: A Memoir of Archbishop Hughes, 1838-1858," *Records and Studies*, XXXIX-XL (1952), 129-90. Hereafter cited as "Memoir."

[57]*Ibid.*, 135-162 *passim*.

[58]*Ibid.*, 136. Although the trustee system was not an evil *per se*, its use had resulted in scandals during the 18th and 19th centuries in a number of dioceses, including Philadelphia where Hughes had served from 1827-38.

[59]*Ibid.*, 137-39. The system, however, continued to be a problem in Buffalo even after that section bcame a separate diocese in 1847.

[60]*Ibid.*, 168-74.

[61]On January 3, 1849, shortly after the news of the Pope's flight to Gaeta reached the United States, Hughes preached in New York's cathedral on "The Present Position of Pius IX." Lawrence Kehoe (Ed.), *Complete Works of the Most Reverend John Hughes, D.D., Archbishop of New York* (New York, 1866), I, 11-21. Hereafter cited as *Hughes*.

⁶²Browne, "Memoir," *loc.cit.*, 178-180. In the municipal election of 1858 in Baltimore, the American Party candidate won because it was too dangerous for the Democrats to support their candidate; New Orleans' Democrats claimed that they were defeated in 1857 because of violence and fraud; nativism in Louisville was reinforced when a convention there in 1858 drew up nativist resolutions. *Cf.* Sister M. St. Patrick McConville, *Political Nativism in the State of Maryland, 1830-1860* (Washington, D.C., 1928), 121; William D. Overdyke, *The Know-Nothing Party in the South* (Baton Rouge, 1950), 283-86; Sister Agnes McGann, *Nativism in Kentucky to 1860* (Washington, D.C., 1944), 86-113.

⁶³Kehoe, *Hughes*, 686-701.

⁶⁴Lyman, *op.cit.*, 94-105 *passim*; *Dolan*, op.cit., 12.

⁶⁵James H. Callender, *Yesterdays in Little Old New York* (New York, 1929), 122-131.

⁶⁶Edward Pessen, "Political Democracy and the Distribution of Power in Antebellum New York City," in Irwin Yellowitz (Ed.), *Essays in the History of New York City* (New York, 1978), 35ff.

Chapter II (pp. 25-47)

[1]Leo Hershkowitz, *Tweed's New York, Another Look* (New York, 1977), 39-40.

[2]*Ibid.*, 47-61.

[3]New York's Central Park (59th to 110th Streets, Fifth Avenue to Central Park West) was America's first major urban park in a picturesque setting. It is also the only municipal park that is a national historic landmark. John Tauranac, *Essential New York, A Guide to the History and Architecture of Manhattan's Important Buildings, Parks and Bridges* (New York, 1979), 46-47; Hershkowitz, *op.cit.*, 42.

[4]In 1855 only five Blacks voted, for most were unable to meet the stiff property qualifications. Hershkowitz, *op.cit.*, 42.

[5]Kehoe, *Hughes*, II, 270.

[6]This site had earlier Catholic associations. The literary institution, established by Father Anthony Kohlmann, S.J., in 1808, was moved in 1810 to the block between Fourth and Fifth Avenues and 50th and 51st Streets. It flourished there until it was ordered closed in 1813 by the Jesuit Superior of the Maryland Mission, Father John Grassi, because the Fathers were needed to keep Georgetown College going. In September, 1813, the Trappist monks opened an orphan asylum in the house the Jesuits had used. Smith, *op.cit.*, I, 45. *Cf.* Timothy J. Riordan, "St. Peter's Sesquicentennial Celebration," *Records and Studies*, vol. 26, 26-27; Meehan, *loc.cit.*, 123.

[7]Trustees Minutes, vol. 1, November 3, 5, 6, 10 and 18, 1828. In 1842 the trustees conveyed a portion of this land on the northeast corner of 50th Street, east of Madison Avenue, for the purpose of erecting the Church of St. John the Evangelist. Later, this land was sold under foreclosure and Hughes eventually purchased it and conveyed title to the cathedral trustees.

[8]*Ibid.*, August 12 and 29, 1832.

[9]*Ibid.*, vol. 3, December 8, 1852.

[10]*Ryan, op.cit.*, 200.

[11]Trustees Minutes, vol. 3, February 2, 10, March 22, 1853.

[12]It was here that the cathedral trustees purchased an out-of-town house for Hughes when, in 1853, he indicated his preference for the "house and ground belonging to Mr. Spalding at Manhattanville," Trustees Minutes, vol. 3, June 27,1853. Since the archbishop rarely used it, the property was sold and a house on the northwest corner of 36th Street and Madison Avenue was purchased and Hughes moved from the Mulberry Street residence to Madison Avenue, spending the last decade of his life there and sharing the house with his sister, Mrs. William Rodrigue, her husband and their children. Meehan, *loc.cit.*, 139ff.

[13]Hershkowitz, *op.cit.*, 35.

[14]Lloyd Morris, *Incredible New York* (New York, 1951), 11; Edward Robert Ellis, *The Epic of New York* (New York, 1966), 277. Hereafter the latter work will be cited as: E.R. Ellis, *Epic.*

[15]E. R. Ellis, *Epic.*, 272.

[16]Richard Bowe, *The New York City Story* (New York, 1963), 31.

[17]Richard Shaw, *Dagger John* (New York, 1977), 109.

[18]Walter Knight Sturges, "Renwick, Rodrigue and the Architecture of Saint Patrick's," Cathedral Bulletin, *Alive and Well and Living in New York City*, February 1980, 12-13.

[19]Trustees Minutes, vol. 3, June 2, 1858.

[20]Farley, *St. Patrick's Cathedral*, 119; Kehoe, *op.cit.*, II, 264.

[21]Kehoe, *op.cit.*, II, 269-270.

[22]Farley, *St. Patrick's Cathedral*, 121. Kehoe, *op.cit.*

[23]Trustees Minutes, vol. 3, June 2, 1858.

[24]Farley, *St. Patrick's Cathedral*, 121.

[25]Hughes to Smith, June 16 and September 10, 1858, cited in Farley, *St. Patrick's Cathedral*, 122, 123, 126.

[26]Kehoe, *op.cit.*, II, 263.

[27]These two were New Yorkers who had traveled in Europe and wished to see "at least one ecclesiastical edifice on Manhattan Island of which their native city will have occasion to be proud." Kehoe, *op.cit.*, II, 267.

[28]Although several attempts have been made over the years, it has not been possible to locate the original cornerstone. In 1965, a Mrs. Georgina Henderson of Ottawa, Canada, wrote to Cardinal Spellman that her father-in-law "did all the plastic work on the Cathedral. My husband . . .thinks he remembers his father saying that the corner-stone was placed under the altar before the installation of a copy of Leonardo da Vinci's "Last Supper." The Cardinal replied, thanking her for her letter but adding "It will be difficult to locate the cornerstone now since an entirely new altar has been erected." AANY, D-3, Spellman to Mrs. Neil Henderson, October 19, 1965. The cornerstone had not been located when, on August 15, 1978, a commemorative ceremony of the 120th anniversary of Hughes' laying of the original cornerstone and the dedication of the "cornerstone of the future" was held. *Cf. Saint Patrick's Cathedral, The 100th Year*, 101-102.

[29]New York *Times*, August 16, 1858.

[30]Farley, *St. Patrick's Cathedral*, 116-119.

[31]E. R. Ellis, *Epic*, 273.

[32]Hershkowitz, *op.cit.*, 40.

[33]Farley, *St. Patrick's Cathedral*, 127.

[34]Hershkowitz, *op.cit.*, 72-73.

[35]*Ibid.*, 73.

[36]Kehoe, *Hughes*, II, 763.

[37]Hughes to Governor William H. Seward, January 29, 1862, John Tracy Ellis, *Documents of American Catholic History* (Milwaukee, 1962), No. 109, 371.

[38]Hershkowitz, *op.cit.*, 91ff.

[39]Kehoe, *Hughes*, II, 548; Shaw, *op.cit.*, 367-69.

[40]Farley, *The Life of John Cardinal McCloskey* (New York, 1918) 199. Hereafter this work will be cited as *McCloskey*.

[41]Farley, *St. Patrick's Cathedral*, 98-99; 133-134.

[42]Farley, *McCloskey*, 66-161 and 210-226 *passim*; Smith, *op.cit.* I, 267-268.

43 Farley, *McCloskey*, 242-320 *passim.*

44 AANY, A-34, "Circular, John, Abp. of New York, Re: Cathedral Debt Fund, New York, Feast of St. Patrick, A.D. 1865."

45 Farley, *McCloskey*, 242-43.

46 AANY, "Account Book of John, Abp. of New York, 7th District." This district covered the area from 40th Street to Spuytendivel [*sic.*] Creek. *Ibid.*

47 John Tracy Ellis, *The Formative Years of The Catholic University of America* (Washington, D.C., 1946), 96-97.

48 AANY, "Account Book of John, Abp. of New York." Church asessments between 1867-1871 totaled some $874,571, while individual donations to February 1871 amounted to $196,463.96, including interest to date at 4%. *Ibid.*

49 Trustees Minutes, Special Meeting, vol. 4, March 16, 1866; July 8, 1873; vol. 5, January 24, 1874; July 26, 1876.

50 AANY, James Lynch, Treasurer, "Cathedral Fair...Daily Deposits made in Central National Bank," October 22 - November 23, 1878, $172,625.48; Farley, *St. Patrick's Cathedral*, 129.

51 *American Architect and Building News*, May 31, 1879.

52 AANY, A-26, "A Catholic American" to His Eminence Cardinal McCloskey, n.d., n.p.

53 E.R. Ellis, *Epic*, 360-61.

54 *American Architect and Building News*, May 31, 1879.

55 William Quinn, Vicar General, *St. Patrick's Cathedral, A Full Description of the Exterior and Interior of the New Cathedral, the Altars and Windows, with Biographical Sketches of His Eminence Cardinal McCloskey and The Most Reverend Archbishop Hughes, D.D.* (New York, 1886), Preface.

56 New York *Times*, May 26, 1879, 5.

57 In 1884, Ryan became Archbishop of Philadelphia, then the second largest diocese in the nation. He preached at the installation of Michael A. Corrigan as third Archbishop of New York (1886), as well as at

Corrigan's twenty-fifth anniversary of consecration (1889) and at his Requiem Mass (1902). Farley, *St. Patrick's Cathedral*, 139, 145, 146.

[58]Farley, *McCloskey*, 346-348. Here, Ryan overlooked the great cathedrals of Mexico City and Lima.

[59]James Renwick to Trustees, October 16, 1888. Trustees Minutes, vol. 7, December 6, 1888.

[60]Eugene Kelly was the founder of a New York City branch bank, Kelly and Company. He had married Margaret Anna Hughes, the archbishop's niece. At his retirement in 1894, he was said to be worth about $15,000,000. John L. Morrison, "Kelly, Eugene," *New Catholic Encyclopedia* (San Francisco, 1967), vol.5, 146. Hereafter cited as *NCE*.

[61]Trustees Minutes, vol.8, May 4, 1899.

[62]Trustees Minutes, vol. 8, January 7, 1904, "Special Report of the Executive Committee on the Story of the Lady Chapel, December 3, 1903."

[63]To the west of this Sacristy, a bronze door opens into the burial crypt of the archbishops of New York. Farley, *St. Patrick's Cathedral*, 165.

[64]Trustees Minutes, vol.8, January 7, 1904, "Special Report...on Story of the Lady Chapel."

[65]Farley, *St.Patrick's Cathedral*, 170.

[66]*Ibid.*, 141.

[67]Robert I. Gannon, *The Cardinal Spellman Story*, (New York, 1962), 267.

[68]Oscar Handlin, *The Newcomers* (New York, 1962), 12ff.

[69]Charles, Lord Russell of Killowen, *Diary of a Visit to the United States in the Year 1883* (New York, 1910), 32-33. Hereafter cited as *Diary*. Russell was not even Sir Charles when he first visited the United States, but came in the party of Lord Chief Justice Bowen. In 1894, he was appointed Lord Chief Justice of England and few English lawyers were admired as much as he, both in America and throughout Europe. *Cf.* "Russell of Killowen, Charles Russell," *Encyclopedia Britannica* (Chicago, 1969), vol. 19, 773-74.

[70]Russell of Killowen, *Diary*, 38, 207, 213, 218.

Chapter III (pp. 48-73)

[1] Farley, *St. Patrick's Cathedral*, 150.

[2] "Right Reverend Monsignor William Quinn," *Records and Studies*, IV (1906), 102; Farley, *McCloskey*, 127, 142-143.

[3] Ryan, *op.cit.*, 198-218 *passim*.

[4] Smith, *op.cit.*, I, 302 ff; Farley, *St. Patrick's Cathedral*, 150-151.

[5] Kate Simon, *Fifth Avenue, A Very Social History* (New York, 1978). Gould's speculation in gold resulted in the panic of "Black Friday" on September 24, 1869, when the price fell sharply, 121, 149, 304; James T. Maher, *The Twilight of Splendor* (Boston, 1975), 275.

[6] Simon, *op.cit.*, 138-211 *passim*.

[7] Russell, *op.cit.*, 36.

[8] Lyman, *op.cit.*, 181-212 *passim*.

[9] Handlin, *op.cit.*, 42ff.

[10] Lyman, *op.cit.*, 223-24.

[11] *Freeman's Journal*, December 10, 1904.

[12] Published in 1890, this work was reprinted in 1972 by Corner House Publishers of Williamstown, Massachusetts. By 1890, the census showed that the population of Manhattan Island had reached 1,440,101. Of these Riis estimated that 1,250,000 lived in tenements, and of this tenement population, an estimated 163,712 were children under five years of age. *Ibid.*, 300, 304.

[13] Joseph L. Hoey, *The Church in the Metropolis...from 1785 to 1896* (New York, 1896), 90.

[14] Smith, *op.cit.*, II, 438.

[15] Farley, *St. Patrick's Cathedral*, 151; Smith, *op.cit.*, 438.

[16] Aubert J. Clark, "Joseph Henry McMahon," *NCE*, IX, 39-40.

[17]Trustees Minutes, v. 2, March 2, 1905.

[18]Smith, *op.cit.*, II, 372-73. The legistlation of the Third Synod pro-mulgated the legislation of the Second Plenary Council of Baltimore, as well as embracing earlier useful synodal legislation. *Ibid.*, 374.

[19]AANY, G-8, John Crane to Archbishop Corrigan, April 15, 16, 1895.

[20]Farley, *St. Patrick's Cathedral*, 133-134.

[21]AANY, C-9, Margaret A. Kelly to Archbishop Corrigan, January 4, 1883.

[22]Bernard J. McQuaid, Bishop of Rochester to Corrigan, May 23, 1883; Farley, *McCloskey*, 354-363 *passim*.

[23]AANY, C-15, Gibbons to Corrigan, October 7, 1885.

[24]Farley, *McCloskey*, 367-368.

[25]*Ibid.*, 364-65.

[26]John Tracy Ellis, *The Life of James Cardinal Gibbons* (Milwaukee, 1952), I, 550-632 *passim*. Hereafter cited as *Gibbons*.

[27]Daniel F. Reilly, O.P., *The School Controversy, 1891-1893* (Washington, D.C., 1943), 160-162 and 1-38. *Cf.* Sister M. Patricia Ann Reilly, O.P., "The Administration of Parish Schools in the Archdiocese of New York, 1800-1900," *Records and Studies*, XLIV, 61-63.

[28]M.P.A. Reilly, *loc.cit.*, 64.

[29]D.F. Reilly, *op.cit.*, 158-159; 271-276; 226-230.

[30]Maurice Francis Egan, *Recollections of a Happy Life* (New York, 1925), 133. Egan had served as editor of the New York *Freeman's Journal*.

[31]Robert Emmett Curran, *Michael Augustine Corrigan and the Shaping of Conservative Catholicism in America 1878-1902* (New York, 1978), 356, 402, 403.

[32]J. T. Ellis, *Gibbons*, I, 693.

[33]Smith, *op.cit.*, II, 424-25.

[34]J. T. Ellis, *Gibbons*, I, 591.

[35]Smith, *op.cit.*, II, 554, 429.

[36]ACUA, "Rector's Office Correspondence (1903-1909)," H-L, Michael J. Lavelle to Denis O'Connell, May 5, 1908.

[37]AANY, C-11, "Testimonial Dinner, Delmonico's, May 30, 1886."

[38]AANY, C-11, Quinn to Corrigan, June 18, 1886; December 20, 1886.

[39]"Right Reverend Monsignor William Quinn," *Records and Studies*, IV (1906), 102.

[40]"Michael Joseph Lavelle," *NCE*, VIII, 540-41.

[41]Trustees Minutes, v. 7, December 6, 1888.

[42]AANY, Meta Renwick Sedgwick to Corrigan, June 24, 1895. Renwick was buried from Grace Church and the cathedral trustees attended the services in a body, but Corrigan was "unavoidably prevented" from being present. *Ibid.*, June 25, 1895.

[43]Farley, *St. Patrick's*, 217.

[44]AANY, C-18, Corrigan to Renwick, January 2, 1891.

[45]Archbishopric of New York, *Saint Patrick's Cathedral* (New York, 1942), 49; 53f.

[46]Farley, *St. Patrick's*, 182.

[47]AANY, "Journal of Bishop Farley," December 25, 1899.

[48]*Freeman's Journal*, January 11, 1902.

[49]Clark, *loc.cit.*, 39-40; AANY, C-30, "The Cathedral Library," a pamphlet, (1893?).

[50]AANY, C-30, "The Cathedral Library."

[51]Clark, *loc.cit.*, 40.

[52]*Freeman's Journal*, November 21, 1902.

[53]James Addison White, *The Founding of Cliff Haven* (New York, 1950), 26-27. Hereafter cited as *Cliff Haven*.

[54]*Freeman's Journal*, January 22, 1898.

[55]*Ibid.*, February 14, 1903; January 13, 1906.

[56]*Ibid.*, October 1, 1904, "Report of Commission Appointed by Archbishop Farley"; and November 5, 1904.

[57]Trustees Minutes, vol. 7, November 1, 1894.

[58]*Ibid.*, Lavelle to Trustees, January 3, 1895; January 2, 1896.

[59]AANY, C-19, Lavelle to Corrigan, March 12, 1899; G-20, McMahon to Corrigan, July 6, 1898; *Freeman's Journal*, February 5, 1898.

[60]AANY, G-20, McMahon to Corrigan, June 3, 1901.

[61]AANY, 1-14, McMahon to Bishop John Farley, February 17, 1901.

[62]"Joseph Henry McMahon," *NCE*, vol. 9, 39-40; "Michael Joseph Lavelle," *NCE*, vol. 8, 540-41.

[63]Trustees Minutes, vol. 8, April 16, 1900, Corrigan to Board of Trustees.

[64]*Freeman's Journal*, March 3, 1902 and May 10, 1902.

[65]Farley, *St. Patrick's*, 147.

[66]*Freeman's Journal*, May 10, 17, 1902.

[67]*Ibid.*

[68]New York, *Town Topics*, June 5, 1902, cited in Curran, *Corrigan*, 513.

[69]Farley, *St. Patrick's*, 150.

Chapter IV (pp. 74-94)

[1] Farley, *St. Patrick's Cathedral*, 151.

[2] *The Catholic Directory, Almanac and Ordo* (New York, D. J. Sadlier & Company), 1883, 133.

[3] ANYCB, "History of the Cathedral Community in New York City, 1882-1941." A handwritten chronicle of the major events of each school year of the boys' department of cathedral school kept by a succession of anonymous scribes. Hereafter cited as "History."

[4] The former was known as "Big Brother Austin," the latter as "Little Brother Austin." *Cf.* Brother Angelus Gabriel, F.S.C., *The Christian Brothers in the United States, 1848-1948* (New York, 1949), 184; ANYCB, "History," 4, 9.

[5] ANYCB, "History," 4, 9-12, 17, 27, 33.

[6] Gabriel, *op.cit.*, 319.

[7] Trustees Minutes, v. 14, October 18, 1942.

[8] *The Official Catholic Directory* (New York, P. J. Kenedy & Sons), 1930. Hereafter cited as *Catholic Directory.*

[9] Gabriel, *op.cit.*, 182-3.

[10] ANYCB, "History," 4-6.

[11] Gabriel, *op.cit.*, 587.

[12] ANYCB, "History," 39-42.

[13] *Ibid.*, 14-21.

[14] *Ibid.*, 40-53 *passim.*

[15] Sister Mary Agnes O'Brien, S.C., *History and Development of Catholic Secondary Education in the Archdiocese of New York* (New York, 1949), 116.

[16] Sister Marie de Lourdes Walsh, *The Sisters of Charity of New York, 1809-1959* (New York, 1960), II, 91.

[17] *Freeman's Journal*, July 15, 1897.

[18] George Johnson, "The Catholic Church and Secondary Education," in Roy J. Defarri (Ed.), *Vital Problems of Catholic Education in the United States* (Washington, D.C., 1939), 75.

[19] Walsh, *op.cit.*, II, 91.

[20] O'Brien, *op.cit.*, 117.

[21] *Annual Report of the Board of Regents*, 1911, 364-65; cited in O'Brien, *op.cit.*, 117.

[22] Walsh, *op.cit.*, II, 92-94.

[23] O'Brien, *op.cit.*, 117.

[24] *Ibid..*, 136. This branch library was relocated in the new building with a separate entrance at 564 Lexington Avenue.

[25] Walsh, *op.cit.*, II, 93.

[26] *The Cathedral Bulletin* (December, 1963), 4.

[27] The Washington University opened in November, 1889. *Cf.* John Tracy Ellis, *The Formative Years of the Catholic University of America* (Washington, D.C., 1946). 367ff.

[28] By this time, McMahon was Pastor of Our Lady of Lourdes Church in New York City, while continuing as Director of the Cathedral Library and its programs.

[29] Peter E. Hogan. S.S.J., *The Catholic University of America, 1896-1903: The Rectorship of Thomas J. Conaty* (Washington, D.C., 1949), 84-85.

[30] ACUA, Joseph H. McMahon to Thomas A. Conaty, New York, April 24, 1902.

[31] Hogan, *op.cit.*, 86.

[32] Colman J. Barry, O.S.B., *The Catholic University of America, 1903-1909: The Rectorship of Denis J. O'Connell* (Washington, D.C., 1950), 218.

[33] ACUA, McMahon to Conaty, April 24, 1902.

[34] Barry, *op.cit.*, 219-220 f.n. 98.

[35] James Addison White, *The Founding of Cliff Haven* (New York, 1950), 25-26; 42.

[36] UNDA, "Onahan Papers," Katherine Conway to William J. Onahan, July 15, 1893; cited in White, *op.cit.*, 39.

[37] White, *op.cit.*, 43-44; 49.

[38] Michael V. Gannon, "Before and After Modernism: The Intellectual Isolation of the American Priest," in J.T. Ellis, *The Catholic Priest in the United States, Historical Investigations* (Collegeville, Minnesota, 1971), 333. Hereafter cited as *The Catholic Priest in the United States.*

[39] Driscoll and all but one of the other five Sulpicians on the Dunwoodie faculty severed connections with the Company of Saint Sulpice in 1906 and continued their seminary work as priests of the Archdiocese of New York. *Ibid.*, 106, f.n. 133; 332-334.

[40] The "modernist movement" was more of a spontaneous rather than an organized phenomenon with centers of influence in France, England, Italy and Germany. After *Pascendi*, modernism became "a slogan to be applied to whatever was disliked in liberal Catholic thought, theology, literature and politics." *Cf.* "Modernism," *NCE*, IX, 994-95.

[41] Gannon, *loc.cit.*, 341-42. In 1909, Driscoll was removed from the rectorship at the seminary, where he was succeeded by the Reverend John P. Chidwick, while Driscoll replaced Chidwick as Pastor of St. Ambrose Church in Manhattan, J.T. Ellis, "The Formation of the American Priest: An Historical Perspective," in *The Catholic Priest in the United States,* 66-67. The two priests, Francis P. Duffy and John F. Brady, who had first conceived the *Review* and then served as associate and managing editors, respectively, did not remain at Dunwoodie very long after Driscoll's departure. Duffy, whose scholarly work ceased in 1908, was named, at his request, pastor of a new church in the Bronx (1912); Brady left in 1910 to assume the vice-presidency of the College of Mt. St. Vincent. *Ibid.*, 347-48.)

[42] *Freeman's Journal*, April 11, 1903.

[43] With the steady encroachment of business establishments in the midtown area, real estate values doubled within a few years. Thus, when the decision was made to move the orphans to a new home in the Kingsbridge section of the city, the block occupied by the boys' asylum, with the

exception of the portion used by the Boland Trade School, was sold to commercial interests in 1899 for $2,050,000. Two years later, the girls' asylum on Madison Avenue sold for $1,200,000. Walsh, *op.cit., III, 11-12.* In 1901, the remaining Boland Trade School property was purchased by the archdiocese for $350,000. *Freeman's Journal,* April 11, 1903.

[44] *Ibid.,* April 19 and September 19, 1903, respectively.

[45] J.T. Ellis, "Cardinal Gibbons and New York," *Records and Studies,* XXXIX-XL (1952), 24.

[46] Smith, *op.cit.,* II, 609.

[47] AAB, 99-Q-3, Gibbons to McMahon, April 23, 1902; cited in Hogan, *op.cit.,* 57.

[48] Barry, *op.cit.,* 261-64; 198.

[49] AANY, Spellman Files, C1, "Lavelle School for the Blind."

[50] Florence E. Gibson, *The Attitudes of the New York Irish Toward State and National Affairs, 1848-1892* (New York, 1951), 316; 320-323. Since the census of 1880 showed that the total population of New York City was 1,206,299, of whom the total of voting males in the city was about 441,505, including some 87, 685 who were Irish born and another 207,486 who were all or in part of Irish ancestry, it was small wonder that an Irishman won the election in 1880.

[51] Walsh, *op.cit.,* II, 68.

[52] *Ibid.,* II, 69-71.

[53] *Catholic News,* LXXVIII, No. 39, September 26, 1963.

[54] Tauranac, *op.cit.,* 93-94. Immigrants who travelled first or cabin class were spared the indignities of Ellis Island since, upon arrival of their ship in the harbor, a cutter brought inspectors who boarded the ship and, after examining their papers and giving them a cursory physical examination, cleared them for debarkation at the dock.

[55] Lyman, *op.cit.,* 196-203.

[56] Simon, *op.cit.,* 224.

[57] Morris, *op.cit.,* 293.

[58] Lyman, *op.cit.*, 235-36.

[59] Ronald H. Bayor, *Neighbors in Conflict, The Irish, Germans, Jews and Italians of New York City, 1929-1941*, (Baltimore, 1978), 42.

[60] In some cases, the assessments amounted to several thousand dollars a day. Simon, *op.cit.*, 158.

[61] Tauranac, *op.cit.*, 57.

[62] Handlin, *Al Smith and His America* (Boston, 1958), 118-120.

Chapter V (pp. 95-122)

[1] "Corrigan to Board of Trustees, New York, April 16, 1900;" Trustees Minutes, vol. 8, April 19, 1900. At this time the mortgage amounted to $270,000, towards which Lavelle agreed to raise $150,000 and the trustees a similar amount on or before January 1, 1904, *Ibid.*, May 3, 1900. Church law requires the consecration of a cathedral, but it first must be debt-free; in the interim, the use of the church is permitted. *Cf.* Bernard J. Comaskey, "Cathedral," *NCE*, III, 247-48.

[2] Trustees Minutes, vol. 8, Special Meeting, September 22 and Adjourned Meeting October 20, 1910. Earlier that year, in April, John D. Crimmins, Treasurer of the Board of Trustees, had noted that since the trustees were "not in possession of income-producing properties, the cemeteries excepted," it would be "proper to expect subordinate parishes in the diocese to contribute to the cathedral's support, and not too much to expect even from the churches in the archdiocese. . . " Recalling that the trustee system in the Church of New York "was abolished years ago," Crimmins added "the Cathedral is the only church of our faith in the city managed by trustees." AANY, 1-13, to Board of Trustees, St. Patrick's Cathedral from John D. Crimmins, April 17, 1910. "The system of lay trusteeism. . . remains to this day in New York's old and new Cathedral of St. Patrick even though elsewhere in the diocese it was eventually abolished." *Ibid.*, Browne typescript of Hughes biography, Chapter V, 39.

[3] "Minute spread upon the records of this meeeting by the trustees to express their appreciation of his [Archbishop Farley] labors and their devotion to his person." *Ibid.*, October 20, 1910.

[4] The College of Cardinals, in conclave, has the exclusive right to elect the pope. Since Vatican Council II, all cardinals, as bishops, participate in the central government of the Church.

[5] In 1911, the exterior of the cathedral was illuminated for the first time as a welcome to Cardinal Farley upon his return from Rome; the floral decorations for the occasion cost $3,500. Trustees Minutes, vol. 9, January 11, February 8, 1912; February 12, 1914.

[6] *Freeman's Journal*, June 2, 1906.

[7] AANY, 0-5, Rachel K. McDowell, "Draft of announcement of expected appointment of Hayes as Archbishop of New York," n.d. The author of this draft describes Hayes as one who "seems to have perfect self-control — and cites as an example his handling of the situation the

day the bomb exploded in the cathedral. At the time, Hayes was at work in the chancery with another priest who "jumped almost to the roof ...but the Bishop did not move a muscle...[but] quietly directed the closing of the Cathedral to the public...arranged other details...and returned to his work."

[8]Trustees Minutes, vol. 9, May 10, 1917.

[9]These figures were derived from the Historical War Records of the National Catholic War Council, preserved on microfilm at the Catholic University of America Archives, Cited in J. M. Butler, "Echoes of the First World War," *Records and Studies*, XXXII (1941), 118ff.

[10]Alfred W. Crosby, *Epidemic and Peace (Westport, Connecticut, 1976), 21, 60-61. Cf.* Thomas Francis, Jr., "Influenza," *Encyclopedia Britannica* (Chicago, 1969), vol. 12, 242-44.

[11]Butler, *loc.cit.*, 119.

[12]Trustees Minutes, Vol. 10, Special Meeting, September 20, 1918.

[13]AANY, 1-25, Teresa O'Donohue to Farley, n.d.

[14]Ida Clyde Clarke, *American Women and the World War* (New York, 1918), 327-328.

[15]AANY, 1-24, Gibbons to Farley, November 21, 1917.

[16]Butler, *loc.cit.*, 116-117.

[17]Roger H. Bayor, *Neighbors in Conflict, The Irish, Germans, Jews and Italians of New York City, 1929-1941* (Baltimore, 1979), 8-9.

[18]When, in 1912, the trustees suggested that a plan for increasing the rental on pews should be considered, Lavelle thought "it was better to go about the matter gradually and...to feel the pulse of the parishioners before such action should be decided upon." Trustees Minutes, vol. 9, December 12, 1912.

[19]*Ibid.*, vol. 10, January 9, 1919.

[20]The surplus, however, never exceeded $2,000 for any single year. *Ibid.*, vol. 10, February 9, 1922, February 14, 1924; vol. 11, December 11, 1924, February 10, 1927, February 9, 1928.

[21]*Ibid.*, vol. 11, February 22, 1925, February 11, 1926, October 8, 1925.

22 *Ibid.*, vol. 11, February 11, 1926, "Lavelle 'to Dearly Beloved Brethren, February 14, 1926."

23 *Ibid.*, vol. 11, February 10, 1927.

24 The sanctuary work and other improvements were executed from designs of the architect Charles D. Maginnis with associate Robert J. Reilly. *Ibid.*, vol. 11 March 10, 1927. *Cf. St. Patrick's Cathedral*, New York (New York, 1942), *passim.*

25 Trustees Minutes, vol. 11, November 18, 1926. The total receipts from all sources as of December 31, 1929 amounted to $686,468.70. "Report of Cathedral Jubilee Improvement Fund A/C," *Ibid.*

26 Until July 1930, the ordinary revenue of the cathedral kept up quite well, dropping after that about 25%; however, it was still sufficient to cover the ordinary expenses. *Ibid.*, vol. 12, February 5, 1931. Moreover, by January 1, 1937, contributions to the Cathedral Jubilee Improvement Fund from all sources totaled $681,621.93. However, since the improvements cost over a million dollars, the balance was secured by loans from the Board of Trustees and bills amounting to $1,002,199 had been paid by the end of 1936. *Ibid.*, vol. 13, January 10, 1936.

27 AANY, U-9-20, "Chancery Office to the Priests of the Diocese, April 17, 1929."

28 *Ibid.*, Radiogram and letter: "Eugene S. Burke, Jr., Rector, North American College, to Hayes," n.d.

29 Katherine Burton, *The Dream Lives Forever, The Story of Saint Patrick's Cathedral* (New York, 1960), 129.

30 AANY, U-9-20, "Testimonial Banquet... Hotel Biltmore, Monday, June 10, 1929, 7:30 p.m., Auspices of Trustees of St. Patrick's Cathedral." *Ibid.*, Lavelle to Hayes, June 13, 1929.

31 Barry, *op.cit.*, 257.

32 *The Catholic News*, November 4, 1884.

33 *Freeman's Journal*, July 15, 1905.

34 For the years ending December 1921, 1924 and 1926, receipts for operating expenses amounted to $98,582, $128,280, and $157,995, respectively, with decreasing surpluses of $1,964, $1,033, and $955 in each

of those years. *Cf.* Trustees Minutes, vol. 10, February 9, 1922; March 7, 1924; vol. 11, February 10, 1927.

[35] *Ibid.*, vol. 12, February 15, 1931. These letters invariably carried the terse signature: M. J. Lavelle, Rector.

[36] Bayor, *op.cit.*, 13-14.

[37] Raymond Vernon, *Metropolis, 1985, An Interpretation of the Findings of the New York Metropolitan Region Study* (Cambridge, Massachusetts, 1960); 136-39.

[38] Richard J. Whalen, *A City Destroying Itself, An Angry View of New York* (New York, 1965), 71, 50.

[39] Burton, *op.cit.*, 139.

[40] Robert I. Gannon, S.J., *The Cardinal Spellman Story* (Garden City, N.Y.), 1962, 107-116.

[41] Trustees Minutes, vol. 11, September 6, October 13, 1938; *The Catholic News*, September 10, 1938.

[42] Gannon, *op.cit.*, 133-135.

[43] *The Catholic News*, LXV, No. 10, October 28, 1950, Centennial Number, 2nd section, 21-C.

[44] Sister M. Natolena Farrelly, *Thomas Francis Meehan (1854-1952), A Memoir* (New York, 1944), 5.

[45] *The Catholic News*, LIV, No. 6, October 14, 1939.

[46] *Ibid.*, No. 7, October 21, 1939.

[47] *Ibid.* Father Hammer and Monsignor Lavelle are still remembered with great affection by those alumni/nae of Cathedral School who gather each November for a Mass at St. Patrick's Cathedral and a Communion Breakfast in a nearby restaurant. Both names were mentioned frequently at the 1981 gathering which was attended by 75 former cathedralites. As the guest of Mrs. Nora Lawlor, Class of 1925, the author had an enjoyable and enlightening day.

[48] *Ibid.*, 3.

49 AANY (no file designation on typescript), "Joseph F. Flannelly ."

50 *Ibid.*; Gannon, *op.cit.*, 144-46. Although a secret consistory was held in Rome in December, 1939, no cardinals were named until after World War II ended. At the consistory called in 1946, Spellman was one of the four American prelates nominated for the College of Cardinals. *Ibid.*, 284.

51 *Ibid.*, 267.

52 For an excellent description of the new high altar and baldachin, and the new altar for the Lady Chapel *Cf. Saint Patrick's Cathedral, New York* (New York, 1942), 85-160.

53 Father Daly had been appointed chaplain of New York's 69th Regiment in 1898, serving until his resignation in 1906 because of poor health. At the time of his resignation he was pastor of St. Malachy's Parish on West 49th Street. *Freeman's Journal,* June 9, 1906.

54 *St. Patrick's Cathedral, New York,* 157-60.

55 Trustees Minutes, vol. 14, October 8, 1942.

56 AANY, Spellman Files, C-3, "A Parishioner to Spellman," n.d.

57 New York *Times,* March 23, 1942.

58 AANY, Spellman Files, C-3, John L. Thomas to Spellman, March 23, 1942.

59 *Ibid.*, D-1, "Biography," typescript, May 1964.

60 Ignacy Jan Paderewski was the first layman to be so honored following his death in New York City in 1941. This Polish patriot, pianist and composer was granted interment in Arlington National Cemetery by President Roosevelt; President John F. Kennedy had a bronze marker placed at the grave site in 1963. *NCE,* v. 10, 858.

61 *Catholic News,* v. LIX, No. 34, April 21, 1945.

62 New York *Times,* May 14, 1959.

63 Trustees Minutes, vol. 14, May 16, 1946.

64 *Ibid.*, vol. 14, May 17, 1945; October 18, 1945.

[65] AANY, C3, "St. Patrick's Cathedral," Maginnis to Spellman, September 20, 1949.

[66] Trustees Minutes, vol. 15, May 22, 1947.

[67] AANY, C-4, "St. Patrick's Cathedral," Rockefeller to Spellman, June 2, 1952.

[68] *Ibid.*, Spellman to Rockefeller, October 27, 1952.

Chapter VI (pp. 123-145)

[1] In the absence of the cardinal, Coadjutor Archbishop of New York J. Francis McIntyre was photographed shaking hands with Vishinsky and Novikof. Gannon, *op.cit.*, 337.

[2] *Catholic News*, LXII, No. 37, Sec. 1, September 7, 1959.

[3] Lyman, *op.cit.*, 264.

[4] Burton, *op.cit.*, 213.

[5] *Cf.* "Societies," *Cathedral Bulletin*, November 1957, 5; December 1963, n.p.

[6] *Catholic News*, LXVI, No. 16, December 8, 1951.

[7] *Cathedral Bulletin*, September 1958, 11-12.

[8] Gannon, *op.cit.*, 271; the list of current Hispanic celebrations was graciously provided by Monsignor James F. Rigney, Rector, to the writer, April 13, 1982.

[9] Trustees Minutes, vol. 16, May 16, 1957. An earlier survey of a 20-block midtown area of skyscrapers, hotels and office buildings had produced an overwhelming mandate for a chapel at Park Avenue and 59th Street. *Cf. Catholic News*, LXXIII, Sec. 1, No. 27, July 5, 1958.

[10] *Alive and Well and Living in New York City*, Bulletin published by the Parish of St. Patrick's Cathedral (New York, 1975-   ), February, 1979, 7. Hereafter cited as *Alive and Well....*

[11] *NCE*, "Fast, Eucharistic," V, 847.

[12] Listed in Appendix II.

[13] *Freeman's Journal*, February 10, 1906; Burton, *op.cit.*, 102.

[14] *Catholic News*, vol. 92, No. 51, December 20, 1979.

[15] The first meeting of the Board of Trustees was held on April 25, 1817 in the vestry room of old St. Patrick's Cathedral with Bishop John Connolly presiding as *ex officio* President. The first elected members included Thomas Stoughton, Andrew Morris, Benjamin Disaubry,

Michael Bannan, David Atkinson, James R. Mullany, Thomas Glover, Anthony Duff, Joseph Idley. Trustees Minutes, vol. 1, April 25, 1817.

[16]Listed in Appendix II.

[17]Trustees Minutes, vol. 16, June 22, 1953; vol. 17, April 17, 1968.

[18]*Ibid.*, vol. 8, June 6, 1903.

[19]*Ibid.*, vol. 11, April 11, May 10, 1929.

[20]AANY, Spellman Files, C-4, "St. Patrick's Cathedral," William T. Greene to Spellman, August, 1954.

[21]*NCE*, Robert F. Hayburn, "Music, Sacred Legislation on," vol. 10, 130ff.

[22]Some members of this choir travel from Westchester, Long Island and New Jersey for rehearsals and performances. *Cf. Alive and Well...*, March, 1980.

[23]*Ibid.*, December, 1979, 7.

[24]*Freeman's Journal*, November 6, 1897.

[25]*Ibid.*, June 3, 1905; Trustees Minutes, vol. 8, May 4, 1905.

[26]*Catholic News*, "Commemorating the Centenary of St. Patrick's Cathedral," May 24, 1979, 81-83.

[27]Interview with Mr. Simeola, February 11, 1982; *Cf.* also *Alive and Well...*, December, 1979, 10.

[28]*The Pope's Visit*, Time-Life Special Report (New York, 1965), 6; 14-49.

[29]For a penetrating analysis of the complex and contradictory signs of "our time of troubles," *cf.* J. T. Ellis, "American Catholicism, 1953-1979: A Notable Change," *Thought*, vol. 54, No. 213 (June 1979), 118ff.

[30]AANY, D-3, Spellman Files, Mrs. John J. Reardon to Spellman, January 18, 1965.

[31]*Ibid.*, Spellman to Mrs. John J. Reardon, February 8, 1965.

[32]*Ibid.*, D-2, Spellman to Admiral D. V. Gallery, June 4, 1965.

33 *NCE*, George F. Tiffany, "Spellman, Francis," vol. 16, 430-31.

34 History reveals that "This has been a fairly constant pattern following ecumenical councils." *Cf.* J. T. Ellis, *American Catholicism*, 2nd Ed., Revised (Chicago, 1969), 250.

35 Archbishop Joseph L. Bernardin, then President of the United States Catholic Conference, expressed concern about the prevalence of what he termed "a new concept of what it means to be a Catholic today." *Time*, "A Church Divided," May 24, 1976, 48.

36 "A Walking Tour of St. Patrick's Cathedral," *Alive and Well...*, August, 1979, 5.

37 *Ibid.*, November, 1978, 8-9; February, 1979, 8-9.

38 As early as 1934, Cardinal Hayes had written to Archbishop Michael Curley of Baltimore to ask "if there is anything we could do in New York towards its [Mother Seton's Cause] advancement." In his reply, Curley indicated that "all the documents...had been sent to the Holy See" but there was "some difficulty about her Baptismal Certificate, and of course miracles have not come forth." Moreover "the Postulator seems to be a kind of a '*niente*' in Rome. I have written...asking for the appointment of Father Coad [*sic*] who knows more about Mother Seton and her Cause than all the Vincentian Fathers put together."

39 Cardinal Cooke and Monsignor Rigney received the award with Mayor Edward Koch and Ralph C. Menapace, the President of the Society making the presentation. *Cf. Alive and Well...*, July, 1981, 7.

40 *Catholic News*, "Commemorating the Centenary of St. Patrick's Cathedral," May 24, 1979, 27.

41 In 1965, Cardinal Spellman, acknowledging a letter he had received from a Mrs. Neal Henderson of Ontario, Canada, thanked her for the information she had relayed regarding the location of the original cornerstone of St. Patrick's. However, he added "it will be difficult to locate the cornerstone now since an entirely new altar has been erected" where the original altar, with the cornerstone underneath, had been. AANY, "Spellman Files," D-3, "St. Patrick's Cathedral," Spellman to Mrs. Henderson, October 19, 1965. On November 1, 1978, at the opening ceremony of the centennial celebration, all New Yorkers were invited to place in the Cornerstone of the Future a written expression of "their hopes and concerns for the future." *Cf. St. Patrick's Cathedral, the 100th Year*, 101.

[42]*Catholic News*, "Commemorating the Centennial of St. Patrick's Cathedral," May 24th, 1979, 29.

[43]*Ibid.*, 47, 51.

[44]*Alive and Well...*, September 1979, 2.

[45]*Ibid.* October 1979, Edwin F. O'Brien, "What Does A Coordinator for a Papal Visit Do?," 7.

[46]George Vecsey, "Jews and Protestants Laud Visit," *New York Times*, October 4, 1979, B2.

[47]*Alive and Well...*, July, 1979, 3.

[48]*Ibid.*, June, 1980, 12.

[49]*Ibid.*, October, 1980, 10.

[50]*Ibid.*, February, 1981, 11.

[51]*Ibid.*, March, 1981, 14.

[52]*Catholic News*, "Commemorating the Visit of Pope John Paul II to the United States," October 18, 1979, Sec. 2, 25 & 27.

[53]*Alive and Well...*, September, 1980, 7, 12.

[54]*Cf.* Harvey A. Siegal, *Outposts of the Forgotten* (New Brunswick, N.J.), 1978, *passim.*

[55]*Alive and Well...*, June 1979, 13.

[56]*Ibid.*, September 1981, 4.

[57]NBC, TV interview the evening of the fire.

INDEX

Balduchin at Christmas

Lady Chapel at Easter

Great Rose Window and Organ

Northwest View of St. Patrick's Cathedral

Michael Glazier, Inc.

1723 Delaware Ave., Wilmington, Delaware 19806